# A Wet Butt

## and a

# Hungry Gut

*A Wet*

*Hungry*

# Butt and a Gut

## BY ELWOOD A. CURTIS

JOHN F. BLAIR, *Publisher*
Winston-Salem, North Carolina

THIS BOOK is respectfully dedicated to the members and friends of Organized Fishermen of Florida, who work diligently to bring the bounties of the sea to the people of America.

# Contents

# 1 ~ Those Early Years

I'VE BEEN AROUND long enough to know that there
are plenty of nuts in the world. I mean the human kind,
like sports nuts, gambling nuts, even stamp-collecting nuts.
Now, I've always been a fishing nut, and sometimes I think
that this is the worst kind. I don't believe any other kind
of nut pursues his hobby more arduously than the fisherman, and once the fishing bug has taken possession of him,
the fisherman becomes hopeless, a completely captivated
nut.

Just to prove my point, let me tell you what happened
one warm August evening when I was fifteen or sixteen
years old.

My folks and I were living at our summer home on High
Hill Beach, a little island community off the South Shore of
Long Island. I was in love, as deeply, as passionately, as sick-
eningly as a teen-age boy can be in love. The object of my
adoration was a pretty, perky, blue-eyed blonde named
Frederica, whom everyone called Fritzie.

Like I said, it was a beautiful, warm summer evening. A
big, full August moon spread a shimmering silver path across
the gently rolling surf. A million billion stars danced and
winked in the heavens, and a gentle, salt-laden breeze ca-
ressed our cheeks as Fritzie and I strolled hand in hand along
the deserted beach. It was a perfect night for lovers, and we
were in love. The world was ours; nothing else mattered but
us two, alone together. Nothing could possibly mar this
evening of ecstasy.

And then it happened. As my lovesick eyes gazed out to sea, I saw a large fish leap out of water just beyond the breakers. Its silver belly flashed in the moonlight; then it disappeared back into the sea with a splash. Almost immediately there was another flash, then another, and another.

"Wow!" I cried, tugging at Fritzie's arm. "Did you see that? Bluefish! A whole school of them, and they're whoppers!"

Without waiting for Fritzie to reply, I turned and raced up the beach towards home, leaving her standing there with her mouth open, too surprised to speak.

I almost tore the front screen door off its hinges in my hurry to get my surf rod and tackle box from the hall closet. In less time than it takes to tell it, I was again racing down the beach towards my beloved Fritzie, but now she was just some fool girl standing in the moonlight with her mouth open. My true love was out there—those blues, leaping, beckoning, tantalizing me to dare come after them. I'd completely forgotten to change my clothes, but white linen suit, white shoes, new shirt and tie—what did they matter? Those fish were out there, and I was the only fisherman lucky enough to be on the beach at the time. I waded out into the surf and made my first cast. The shiny, block tin squid had barely hit the surface when a miniature express train grabbed it and ran for the open sea. I was in Paradise. I was in love— with a school of bluefish!

You can well imagine that the coldest fish on the beach that night, and for many nights thereafter, was Fritzie. She never forgave me, you know. Ended up marrying some dude named Alden, who didn't know a block tin squid from a feather jig. Boy, oh, boy—if he only knew what he was missing!

I realize now how lucky I was to have parents who owned a summer cottage on the ocean front at High Hill Beach. A lot luckier than most kids, I reckon. Back in the twenties, High Hill could be reached only by passenger ferry out of Bellmore. Three ferries in Captain Stevens' fleet made six round trips a day across Great South Bay, carrying passengers and the various assortment of goods and staples needed by the tiny community of fifty or sixty cottages. The hour-long ride on the *Surprise* or the *Bellmore* or the little *Carrie A* was always a delight to us kids, especially when Cap Stevens selected one of us to take the wheel while he collected fares from the passengers. Great South Bay, in those days, was made up of sloughs and shallows, acres of eel grass flats and clam bars, crossed and re-crossed by narrow, winding channels marked by slender birch poles driven into the mud at the channel edge. It was an arduous task to pilot a large, deep-draft boat through those channels, but we boys were up to it. Most of us knew those hidden, devious paths as well as we knew our own living rooms. Whichever one of us was chosen to "take over" by Cap Stevens was some proud kid, let me tell you, though he would affect nonchalance, even boredom, in order to hide his pleasure from the others.

Those narrow channels running through the eel grass and on the edges of the clam flats were literally teeming with fish in those days. Fluke, flounder, kingfish, and a dozen other species of bottom feeders could be found in the quiet, deep holes, while weakfish, blues, and striped bass patrolled the channels and sloughs, darting in and out of the shrimp-laden eel grass, looking for food. It was a fisherman's dream come true—unspoiled, uncrowded, and undisturbed. "Pollution" was a word found only in the dictionary.

All of us young fellows on the beach owned boats of one sort or another. My father had a little sixteen-footer, narrow of beam and shallow of draft, which was powered by a one-cylinder Palmer marine motor. We called her the *Trickey*, and she was just that. Cantankerous, unreliable, wet as all get-out in a choppy sea, she was just about everything a boat should not be, but I loved her and babied her as much as if she had been a sixty-foot yacht. When I proved to my father's satisfaction that I could swim like a fish and could handle my boat and myself safely under almost any conditions, he turned the *Trickey* over to me, accompanied by the usual fatherly admonitions to be careful and behave myself. I guess I was about eight at the time.

I was kind of puny and sickly as a kid, and that little one-cylinder Palmer presented an almost insurmountable problem. It had to be hand cranked to start, and, having magneto ignition, the motor had to be cranked vigorously, else it would spin in reverse and probably break, or at least wrench, your arm if you held on to the little brass cranking handle. I was afraid of the darn thing, I'll admit, but I yearned with all my little-boy heart to take the *Trickey* out all by myself. The solution to my dilemma was my friend Dick Deede, a husky, healthy, well-built kid, who could spin *Trickey's* little Palmer as well as he could spin the heavy-duty Kermath in his own boat. Dick went along with the plan I devised. He'd start the *Trickey*, then I'd throttle her down as far as possible and run past the town dock. Since my boat had no transmission, Dick would have to jump up on the dock while I maneuvered as close to the piling as I could. Then I'd have the *Trickey* all to myself, and I'd head out to the fishing grounds to spend the day. I knew that once I stopped the motor I was stuck out there until it was time to go home. Along about suppertime, I'd pole my way back to the dock. I think it was inevitable that a day of decision would come, and it did. I was fishing for fluke in a deep hole called Diamond Shoals, about a mile and a half from home, when dark, rolling, ominous clouds appeared from nowhere. We were in for a thunderstorm—a humdinger, if I was any judge. I've admitted before that I was afraid of the motor's kick, but I think I was even more afraid of being caught out in the open bay in a bad thunderstorm. I must have tossed a mental coin and decided to take my chances with that little one-cylinder beast. After hauling up the bow anchor, I got the brass crank on the flywheel just right of bottom center and pulled up as hard as I could. The motor turned over—nothing happened. I tried it again—nothing doing.

"Well," I thought, "at least I cranked it, and my arm ain't broke."

Then I noticed I hadn't put the spark plug wire back into the magneto when I'd pulled it out to shut off the motor. I replaced the wire and tried once more. I guess it was a combination of surprise, incredulity, and being off balance that threw me over backwards when the motor started. I landed on my back on the floorboards, but I wasn't hurt. I recovered my feet quickly, grabbed the tiller ropes, and headed for home ahead of the storm. I felt nine feet tall. I'd conquered that cantankerous little Palmer, and I was some proud kid, believe me.

High Hill Beach was a quiet community; it certainly could never be classified as a summer resort or tourist attraction. There were no roads, no sidewalks, not even electricity. A boardwalk running in front of the cottages made them accessible without making it necessary to plod through the deep white sand. The landscape consisted of salt-grass-covered sand dunes, bayberry and dusty miller bushes, and acres of tart, purple, beach plums. It was always pleasantly cool at High Hill, probably fifteen degrees cooler than in the towns and cities "on shore." The prevailing winds in summer were southerly, coming directly across the endless stretches of the Atlantic. On the north side of our community was Great South Bay, extending north to the mainland, east to Fire Island Inlet, and west to Jones Inlet. We residents on High Hill Beach were isolated, and we wanted it just that way.

My parents told the story of the terrible flu epidemic in 1918 or '19, when thousands of folks died from the disease. Father took us to our beach cottage early that year, in late March, I believe. We took along enough provisions to last three or four months, and never once during that time did any of us return to the mainland. There were another half dozen families who had the same idea, and, according to the story my father told, there wasn't a single case of flu on High Hill Beach during the entire epidemic.

The Prohibition Era, referred to by some as the Roaring Twenties, found High Hill Beach a mecca for rum runners who needed isolated caches along the Long Island coast in which to store their cases of liquor before transporting them into New York City. Black-painted speedboats—long, sleek, and shallow of draft, their gunwales almost awash from the heavy loads beneath their floorboards—raced through the inlets, past the watchful eyes of Revenue agents, to the hidden docks and sandy beaches at High Hill. There were fortunes made, literally overnight, by these men who dared flout the Revenue authorities, whose job it was to enforce the unpopular laws of prohibition. Yes, indeed, fortunes were made, but the rum runner who was wise enough to save his money was the exception rather than the rule. It was easy come, easy go, and the majority of those engaged in the illegal rum traffic died broke. In those days at High Hill, the names of men like the Zaccharino brothers, Dudly Mc-Cabe, and Wally Baker were household words. Today, for those who remember, those names are legendary.

Of course, among us kids, the men with the black boats were admired, even worshiped as heroes. I recall quite vividly being invited to go for a moonlight ride on Wally Baker's "fishing boat," a thirty-two-foot, black-hulled sea skiff, powered by two sixteen-cylinder Cadillac motors. Wally was a friend of my father and mother. He was a handsome man in his early thirties, who lived with his wife Betty in a little beach cottage not far from our house. The Bakers had no children, but the little attentions and ready smiles they had for us beach kids endeared them to all of us.

High Hill Beach had a Coast Guard station set back in the sand dunes, away from the beach cottages. It was rumored among the residents that the biggest cache of illegal booze was hidden in a cellar that had been dug for that purpose by the Coastguardsmen themselves. They had elicited Federal funds to have a deep-water canal dug from the open bay to the back yard of the Coast Guard station. This canal was used mostly at night—by the long, sleek boats painted black.

At this point, I believe I should make it clear that there was very little roaring at High Hill during the "Roaring Twenties." There was no violence, highjacking, gangland killings, or armed thugs lurking in the shadows. In fact, none of those activities occurred at High Hill which the public usually associates with that era when illegality was king. The men engaged in the rum traffic were businessmen, most of them family men, who conducted their business quietly, accepting their risks stoically because it was all part of the game.

We boys on High Hill, being prone to hero worship like most kids our age, wanted to grow up to be just like the men at the Coast Guard station. Theirs was the perfect life, or so it seemed to us. They rowed their longboats up and down the bay channels each day, just for the exercise, and they owned a horse—the only horse on the beach, in fact. The Coastguardsmen took turns riding bareback along the surf when they were on patrol, and lucky indeed was the kid who happened to be at surfside when the mounted patrolman came by. Invariably, with a lot of begging and a little cajoling, he could hitch a ride on the horse's back, sitting behind the patrolman, holding on for dear life. The beast couldn't be considered a race horse by any stretch of the imagination; he (or perhaps it was a she) was more the plow-horse variety, big footed, slightly swaybacked, perpetually sleepy, and in constant need of gentle prodding to keep him going at all.

There was a purpose in the Coast Guard keeping him in oats and fodder. About once a week the men would have "rescue drill." A longboat was kept on the ocean front, pulled up on the beach a few hundred yards above high water mark. When a drill was scheduled (and invariably it would be on a beautiful, warm day when the sea was calm), the Coastguardsmen would launch the longboat through the surf, row up and down in front of the beach cottages for an hour or so, then return to shore through the breakers. The launching process was accomplished by means of planks and rollers laid on the soft sand, with the old plow horse hitched to the bow. By the concerted efforts of the horse pulling, the crew pushing, and us kids shouting encouragement, the boat would finally be launched. The return to shore and the stowing of the boat until the next drill was accomplished by the same procedure in reverse. It seems to me that the rescue operation was never called upon in an actual emergency—not in my time, anyway. Ships just didn't crack up and sink off High Hill Beach. With a rescue force such as we had, they wouldn't dare!

There was one occasion, though, when the men at the Coast Guard station did themselves proud. They cut at least thirty minutes off their launching time because they practically picked up their clumsy longboat and ran with it into the sea. Father and I were out fishing that day, so we missed all the fun. The neighbors, though, told us all about it when we got home.

Around midmorning, two fast cutters were spotted about a half mile offshore, racing at full speed, one in pursuit of the other. The lead boat was a rum runner; the pursuer was a Revenue cutter. Just about every High Hill resident ran to the shore to watch the race. The Revenue cutter was gaining, inch by inch, foot by foot. The rum runner would surely be caught unless he took drastic measures right then and there. Apparently he decided to make the supreme sacrifice. The folks on the beach watched, fascinated, as the crew started heaving case after case of liquor over the side. The Coastguardsman on duty in the watchtower followed the race with his binoculars. When he saw the whiskey cases being thrown overboard, he gave the signal to the other men for the rescue operation to begin—but not to rescue the boats or the men aboard them. They beat all previous records for launching in order to rescue the liquor! They were successful, to a limited extent, but case after case drifted ashore, to be grabbed up and hidden away by the spectators. For months thereafter, there was whiskey hidden all over the beach—in outhouses, among roof rafters, beneath boardwalks—in just about every unlikely place the ingenious minds of our residents could imagine. If you think that Father was left out of this bonanza because we were out fishing, you are wrong. He ended up with his share by donations from friends who were willing to divide the fruits of happenstance.

For several days thereafter there was a newcomer among the businessmen who commuted daily on the ferry from High Hill to Bellmore. This newcomer to the commuting set was no stranger; Charlie Hazzard had been a summer resident at High Hill for many years. The folks didn't like Charlie particularly. He kept to himself most of the time, spoke rarely, and was too unsociable to mingle with the other men on the beach or join in with their banter and horse-play. Charlie looked like an undertaker. His gaunt face, sallow cheeks, and lacklustre eyes, to say nothing of his dead-black, wrinkled suit and high starched collar, gave him the appearance of death warmed over.

There were several things about Charlie that annoyed and puzzled the commuters. For one thing, he always sat alone, speaking to no one. At first, some of the men invited him to join them in their usual pinochle game, but when he refused with a grunt, rather than a polite excuse for not joining in, they gave up. For another, there was a black satchel that Charlie carried aboard the ferry each morning and clenched tightly in his lap throughout the hour-long journey across the bay. What was in that satchel old Charlie held on to so tightly? The men wondered, and got more and more curious.

Finally, my father, who was among the daily commuters, came up with an idea as to how they could resolve their curiosity with Charlie none the wiser. Father was a dentist, and a darn good one, if I may say so. Just about every resi-dent on the beach had been his patient at one time or an-other, either in his office in Hicksville or, if a toothache became intolerable and needed to be tended to immediately, in a high-backed rocking chair on the front porch of our beach house. Father whispered his plan to his fellow conspira-tors, then left the group to take a seat next to Mr. Hazzard.

"Well, Charlie," Father exclaimed in his friendliest man-ner, "how are you these days? Don't believe we've had a chance to chat since you were in my office last summer."

"I'm tolerable, Doc, just tolerable," Charlie answered.

"Glad to hear it, Charlie. By the way, are you having any trouble with that tooth I filled for you last year?"

"Not a bit, Doc," Charlie answered firmly. "Feels fine, just fine."

"That reminds me, Charlie," Father said, earnestly, "seems to me you had another tooth in there that wasn't in very good shape. I believe I mentioned it to you at the office. Now, before it starts giving you real trouble, suppose you let me look at it. Only take a minute; won't cost you anything to let me look at it."

When Charlie hesitated, Father took him firmly by the arm. "Come over here in the gangway, Charlie. The light's better. Just leave your satchel there on the seat."

Before Charlie could protest, Father escorted his patient to the shaft of light streaming through the open stairway.

"That's right, Charlie," Father's voice was solicitous. "Only take a second."

Father sat Charlie in a chair so that his back was to the cabin and the other commuters. Father stood back of Charlie, then said, "Now, open wide, Charlie."

Meanwhile, Father's friends crowded around the abandoned satchel. It was Fred Hawkins who stealthily opened the snap locks. The men's suspicions as to the contents were well founded. Inside the satchel were six quarts of whiskey, each bottle carefully wrapped in newspapers. The men nudged one another, grinning. They quickly emptied the satchel of its contraband contents, then proceeded to substitute short lengths of pipe, a worn-out water pump—anything with weight that they could find beneath the seats or in the boat's footlockers. Each piece was wrapped carefully in newspaper to prevent any telltale metallic clinking which might alert Charlie as to what had taken place. When the satchel had been returned to its place on the seat, Fred Hawkins walked to where Father was bent over his patient and gently nudged him. Father knew he could release Charlie—the dastardly deed was done!

It was hard to tell whether Charlie ever discovered that Father was as guilty as the rest of the conspirators. Suffice it to say that that was the last trip old Charlie ever made with the little black satchel.

Father and I were very close during my youth. It was from him that I inherited my love for the sea, the beach, and, most of all, fishing. He had spent his youth on the New Jersey coast in the little beach community of Point Pleasant. As Father told it, he was too poor to afford the luxury of a motorboat, or even a sailboat, so he took pride and pleasure in a rowboat his father bought for him. Father loved to fish. Whenever the opportunity offered during the summer months, he would get up before daylight, launch his rowboat through the breakers, and row out to the fish pound nets, about a mile or so offshore. Father would tie up to one of the pound stakes and drop his baited drop-lines into the net pockets. I suppose one might say Father's bait had a captive audience.

There was one story in particular that Father loved to tell. One day he had launched his boat and rowed out to sea, but instead of tying up to the fish pound stakes, as he usually did, he decided to go further out to fish around the bell buoy, about three miles offshore. He had been fishing for an hour or so when suddenly a boom of thunder rolled across the water from the direction of the shore. The first boom was followed by another, then another, and, almost immediately after each explosion, some heavy, unseen object would splash into the sea several yards from the rowboat. As Father used to tell it:

"Young and dumb as I was, I soon realized I'd anchored my boat in the middle of the Fort Monmouth firing range. I skedaddled for home just as fast as I could row. I figured the Atlantic Ocean just wasn't big enough for both me and those cannon balls. There was no harm done, though, 'cept I scorched the bottom of my rowboat by rowing so fast."

Father taught me a great deal about boat-handling and fishing. The only trouble was, the time we spent together on the water was limited to weekends and his Thursdays off. Therefore, a large portion of my training was gained from an old bayman named Fred Klemm. Fred was all-around handyman for Mrs. Williams, a short, dumpy, piano-legged woman in her sixties who owned the general store on High Hill Beach. Everyone loved Mrs. Williams, though her store prices were outrageous, her merchandise often shopworn, and, more often than not, the commodity you'd just run out of and needed most, she didn't have in stock. Mrs. Williams' thin, stringy hair was dyed henna, though the intensity of the color varied from week to week. We kids were fond of the old lady. She catered to us shamelessly with cookies, candy, and the like. We were very curious as to just what relationship existed between her and Fred Klemm, and I believe the only time I ever saw Mrs. Williams really angry was the day one of us got up nerve enough to ask her if she and Fred were married. The poor old soul's face turned as red as her hair. She grabbed up a shiny new axe handle and chased that kid down the boardwalk all the way to the bay! You couldn't really blame the kid, though. Mrs. Williams and Fred were constantly arguing and fighting, just like married folks.

I guess Mrs. Williams and Fred had been together a long time—since the time when Mr. Williams was still alive. Back in the twenties, the Williamses and Fred operated the Brandt House, a sort of hotel and hunting lodge on an island near Jones Inlet. The Brandt House catered to wealthy sportsmen from the city who'd come out to the lodge to hunt, fish, and just get away from cars, telephones, and business problems for a while. Fred used to tell the story about a party of sports, as he called them, who reserved rooms at the lodge for a weekend and stipulated that they expected to be served wild duck for supper the evening they arrived. Unfortunately, the ducks had already left Great South Bay for parts unknown, but Mrs. Williams had no intention of losing a party of six because of the whim of those unpredictable ducks. Consequently, the day before the party was to arrive, she sent Fred out with his shotgun and instructions to "get me some birds." Fred did. He brought back six sea gulls. As in all good stories, all's well that ends well; the sports ate the sea gulls with gusto and relish and never knew the difference. That's what Fred said, anyway.

You might say Fred Klemm was a typical bayman, if there is such a thing as a typical anything. He was tall and skinny, persimmonous in disposition, cranky and out of sorts most of the time, and lazy to the point of shiftlessness. He loved to argue about anything, with anyone silly enough to argue back, because Fred always won the argument. Even if he lost, he won, because arguing meant he had to stop whatever he was doing before the argument began just to concentrate on repartee.

One day I entered Mrs. Williams' store and was greeted by what sounded like a real knock-down, drag-out argument going on in the back room. I walked behind the counter into the living quarters, and there were Fred and his brother Frank, both pacing back and forth the length of the narrow living room, shouting at each other, their arms flailing the air.

"How can you be so dumb?" cried Fred. "Of all the stupid jackasses I ever seen, you take the cake. Stupid, that's what you are—just plain stupid!"

"I ain't stupid," shouted Frank, defensively, waving his arms. "It's you is stupid. You don't know a bargain when you see one. I done right, no matter what you say. I got a good deal, but you're too dumb to see it!"

By this time I was filled with curiosity, and when both men paused for breath and stood glaring at each other, I entered into the conversation.

"Hey, you guys, what's this all about? Why the big argument?"

Fred turned to me and said in disgust, "I'll leave it up to you, sonny. Is my brother a jackass or ain't he? I told him and told him not to pay more than three dollars for that new, secondhand Ford he got, and here he went and paid five for it! Nobody in his right mind would pay that much for a secondhand car!"

"Well," I said with a straight face, trying to sound philosophical, "what's done is done, though it does seem a heap of money to spend just for a car. Maybe if you quit arguing with Frank he'll take us for a ride someday so we can judge it firsthand."

Actually, Frank did get a bargain. He drove that five-dollar Ford for almost two years without putting a dime's worth of repairs into it. After two years, though, it lay down and died, just like the Wonderful One-Hoss Shay.

Fred and Frank were very much alike, both in disposition and in lack of ambition. In fact, they even looked so much alike it was difficult for some people to tell them apart. Frank, though, was married, and, before his operation, he and his wife had had three children. After his operation (they removed one of his testicles), he had sired four more. This helped identify one brother from the other. I once heard a conversation between two cottage owners that went like this:

First cottage owner: "Have you seen Frank Klemm lately?"

Second C.O. "I'm not sure. Which one is Frank?"

First C.O. "Oh, you know—the one who had one of his whatcha-ma-call-its cut off."

Second C.O. "Oh, THAT one! Nope—haven't seen him."

As far as I know, Fred Klemm still had all his attachments, though he did suffer from a peculiar ailment. He could never get his feet wet without suffering severe leg cramps when he went to bed at night. For this reason, he always wore knee-length rubber boots and never waded in water more than calf deep. Fred said he couldn't even wash his feet, the resulting cramps would be so painful.

Most baymen seem to have an allergy to water. Old Buffie Seaman, a clam-digger and eel-skinner, lived on a dilapidated houseboat which he kept tied up at the High Hill Beach dock during the summer months. Buffie would roam the grass flats at night in his little duck boat, spearing eels and fish by the light of a Coleman lantern. During the day he'd sit on the stern deck of his houseboat skinning eels. He could peel off an eel's skin as easily as I could take off my socks, ending with a snap and a flourish that I envied and admired. No matter how often I practiced, I was never able to skin an eel quite like Buffie did. Perhaps today eel-skinning is a lost art.

Anyway, one summer I noticed Buffie's houseboat was not moored in its usual place at the dock.

"Where's old Buffie?" I asked Fred. "Isn't he coming to the beach this year?"

"Not likely," Fred answered, shaking his head. "Buffie died last winter."

"Gosh, that's awful. How did it happen, Fred?"

"Well," Fred answered slowly, gazing out over the shimmering waters of the bay, "seems like Buffie took sick, and that damn fool sister of his took him to the hospital. First thing they did was give old Buffie a bath. He died."

In the years that Fred and I were fishing companions on Great South Bay, he taught me many things that I have never forgotten. I learned where the best holes were to catch fluke, where the big, tide-running weakfish patrolled the

channels at night, and which clam flats were best for littlenecks, which yielded the most chowder clams. But best of all,
Fred taught me to respect the open bay, with its swirling
eddies and treacherous cross-tides. He taught me to respect
the bounties of nature, never allowing me to take more fish
or clams or eels than I could use. I learned to find hidden,
unmarked channels and to find safe haven for myself and
my boat when sudden summer squalls came up out of nowhere and churned a placid bay into boiling froth. Fred
taught me how to take care of my cranky little *Trickey*,
both while she was in use and after she was pulled up on the
beach for the winter.

There was a saying Fred had which I'll never forget.
Whenever I'd admire a big, fancy yacht making her way
through the winding channels, Fred would say, "You ain't
got no need for a boat like that, sonny. Can't catch no more
fish from a big boat than you can from a rowboat; maybe
less. And always remember," he'd add, "big boat, big trouble; little boat, little trouble." I didn't agree with old Fred
at the time, but now I do.

My first venture into "commercial" fishing occurred when
I was about twelve. My two chums, Dick Deede and Mush
Hournau, joined me in the *Trickey* for almost daily excursions out to the fishing grounds. Hardly a day went by that
we didn't come in with a dozen or so nice big fluke. Of
course, we were bringing in far more than any of our families could use; in fact, our mothers begged us not to bring
another fish home for at least the rest of the season. One of
us, I think it was Mush, came up with a brilliant idea. Why

not sell the fish to the other cottagers? Dick and I readily agreed. It was an easy task to clean our catch, the three of us working together, and, of course, the thought of all the money we would make made the task that much easier. When the fluke were cleaned, we wrapped each one carefully in wax paper, weighed them on Dick's mother's baby scale, and loaded them into my express wagon. We stopped at each house along the boardwalk, and there was hardly a time when we had any fish left after stopping at about a third of the cottages. We sold our catch for twenty cents a pound, and at the end of the first few days we found we were rolling in money. We called ourselves the Can't Catchem Fish Company and appointed Mrs. Williams our treasurer. At the end of each day we would march proudly into Mrs. Williams' store, plunk our day's take upon the counter, and stand by, grinning from ear to ear, as Mrs. Williams, with much ceremony and many flourishes, deposited our bills and coins in the coffee can that stood on the shelf behind the counter. Fred had elaborately scrolled and lettered the sign that was pasted on the front of the can. It read: "Property of the Can't Catchem Fish Co."

We prospered all right, and consequently branched out. We would fish the high tides; then, on low tide, we'd jump overboard on the clam flats and tread hard clams for a few hours. The clams sold as readily as our fresh-caught fish. Chowder clams brought us fifteen cents a dozen; littlenecks, twenty cents. It had been previously agreed upon that Labor Day would be divvy-up day, the day that the Can't Catchem Fish Company would disband for the season. We were ecstatic when the contents of the coffee can in Mrs. Williams' store was divided into three equal shares. Dick, Mush, and I had each earned about thirty-five dollars—a small fortune indeed for twelve-year-olds!

It was the next year that, quite by accident, I entered into another phase of commercial fishing. I was down at the dock, cleaning up and making minor repairs to the *Trickey*, when a well-dressed, middle-aged stranger stopped on the dock to watch me work. After a few moments he spoke:

"Say, kid, are there any fish out there in the bay?"

"Sure are, mister—lots of them," I answered.

"Ever catch any?"

"Caught lots of them. Get a few 'bout every time I go out."

"What kind do you catch?"

"Fluke, mostly. Weakfish, too."

"Know where I can hire a boat and guide?"

"Sure do. You can hire me—and this boat."

"How much will you charge?"

I hesitated a moment. I figured I had a live one and didn't want to scare him off. I tried to sound nonchalant.

"Five bucks—that's for all day. Bait included."

"Suppose we don't get any fish?" I think there was a twinkle in his eye when he asked.

"In that case, don't pay me."

"O.K. It's a deal. When can we go?"

"Tomorrow morning, seven o'clock."

"I'll be here." He grinned broadly as he walked away.

My first charter! I was so excited that I don't think I slept a wink that night.

The fishing trip went well the next day. My charter showed up on time, the *Trickey* ran beautifully, and the fluke were hungry. By the end of the day, we had twelve nice big fluke aboard, and my charter, Mr. Franklin, seemed satisfied. He returned to the dock tired, hungry, and sunburned to a lobster red, but he paid me my five dollars (and a little extra), so I was satisfied, too.

There were several other chartered expeditions that summer. I made a little sign which I placed conspicuously on the *Trickey*'s engine hatch. It read:

Charter Fishing Boat
Five Dollars A Day
Bait Supplied
No Fish—No Pay

I'll admit there were days when I wasn't so sure I'd get my money, especially when I had a party of landlubbers aboard who couldn't catch a fish if someone threw it to them. On those occasions I'd resort to the drop-line I kept stashed away under the seat. I'd quietly drop the baited hook overboard, set the hook into the first fluke that bit, then turn to my party and say, "Beg pardon, but would one of you mind pulling in this line for me? Feels like I snagged something on the bottom."

One of the party would obligingly pull in the drop-line, and I'd feign complete surprise when the "snag" turned out to be a big fluke. Most of the time they'd say it was my fish, since it was caught on my line, but I'd insist they'd caught it, so it belonged to them. When it came to deciding between the fish and five dollars, my decision was never a very difficult one.

The year 1927 marked the end of an era and the begin-

ning of a new one at High Hill Beach. The townships of
Oyster Bay and Hempstead, from which the High Hill
residents leased their homesites, gave the land to the State of
New York, and thus the Long Island State Park Commission
was born. Great South Bay was dredged here and filled
there so that a causeway could be built from Wantagh to
the beach. It seemed almost overnight that Jones Beach
State Park sprang up about two miles west of High Hill.
Progress had set in; there was nothing we could do to stop it.
The Jones Beach Causeway continued eastward, past High
Hill Beach, and extending all the way to Fire Island Inlet.
We were caught up in the development, getting improve-
ments that I, at age twelve, would gladly have done without.
Now we had a roadway to and from the mainland. The
ferry was put out of existence. Could anyone fail to miss
that hour-long, winding, leisurely boat ride, where the
smell of salt and marsh, the feel of spray and sun, conspired
to relax both the bodies and the minds of the passengers?

Gone were the winding channels, the eel grass, the clam
flats. The State dredged deep, creating swift-running waterways from Jones Inlet to Fire Island. The grass flats that
were not dredged were torn out by the fast-running tides.
Much of the feeding grounds upon which the fluke, weakfish, striped bass, and other species of fish depended was
destroyed in the name of progress.

With the installation of electricity, the people of High
Hill put away their kerosene lamps, to be used again only in
case of a power failure. Willie Kyle, the village lamplighter,
no longer had to walk the boardwalk each evening with his
ladder and wind protector to light the kerosene lamps that
illuminated the way with their soft, yellow glow.

A huge, cinder-covered parking field was created at High Hill, and, for the first time, mothers had to caution their children to watch out for cars and to be careful in crossing the highway.

High Hill Beach did not grow, however, in either size or population. The land was not for sale, and no more leases were granted; therefore, no building of additional houses was permitted. Actually, the creation of Jones Beach State Park marked the beginning of the end of High Hill. The residents were notified that the leases on their homesites would not be renewed. By 1940, the houses would have to be moved from State land (at the cottage owners' expense), or the State would burn them down. Today, there is no physical evidence that High Hill Beach ever existed.

For me, the only advantage the causeway brought was the increased accessibility to my beloved beach and fishing. Now, during early spring and late fall, I could beg, cajole, or plead with my father or older sister to drive me and one or two of my friends to the beach on weekends to fish or roam the seashore to our hearts' content. My mother usually had the final say as to whether or not we'd be taken to the beach on a particular day in the off season. Usually, if the thermometer read thirty-two degrees or higher, we were allowed to go. Of course, our fishing activities were confined to the new State Park dock or to the shore, since the *Trickey* was pulled up on the beach and turned over during the winter months. My companions on these weekend expeditions were Eddie Kunz and Sam Collins, boys my own age with whom I went to school. Both Eddie and Sam were almost as crazy about fishing as I was.

# 2 ～ The Trickey II

THE YEAR 1932 was one I shall long remember. For my Christmas and birthday present that year (I was sixteen), my Uncle Charlie, my mother's brother, promised to supply the material and help me build any type of boat I wanted. Uncle Charlie owned a sash and blind factory in Hicksville; he had the space, lumber, and wood-working machines needed for such a project. It was not difficult to pick out the boat I wanted. *Rudder* magazine had blueprints and specifications for an eighteen-foot Cape Cod dory. She was wide of beam, built for rough weather, slow, safe, and dependable. To me, she was the perfect fishing boat.

Thus, during that winter and spring, the *Trickey II* was born. Oh, she was a sturdy boat all right—lapstraked in white cedar, with white oak ribs and bottom planks and cypress deck and trim. I worked on every square inch of her; I knew every rivet, every screw she contained. She was more than just a boat; she was a big part of me. Even before she was launched, it was love at first sight.

The *Trickey II* was powered by a twelve-horsepower Fay & Bowen marine motor—power enough to push her through the water at about eight knots. When the *Trickey II* was about three years old, the Fay & Bowen was replaced by a forty-horsepower Model A Ford conversion. The bigger, more powerful motor did not increase her speed very much; the hull of a Cape Cod dory is just not built for speed. Most of the time I ran at about two-thirds throttle, but it was a good feeling to have the extra power I could call upon in a swift-running tide or head wind.

With the larger, safer, more comfortable new boat, I continued taking out parties for bay fishing. My price of five dollars a day and my policy of no fish—no pay still held, as did my little trick with the drop-line, so my parties seldom, if ever, came home "skunked."

Zachs Bay, located on the north side of Jones Beach, was dredged by the State Park Commission as a haven for yachts belonging to visitors to Jones Beach. During the summer months, especially on weekends, the yacht basin would be filled to capacity, accommodating as many as three hundred boats of every imaginable size and description. This was a potential gold mine for an enterprising teen-ager with a boat, and I took full advantage of it. Groceries, ice, and liquor were in great demand among the yachtsmen; the only store within eight miles of the basin was Mrs. Williams' store on High Hill. I conceived the idea of going from yacht to yacht with the *Trickey II*, taking orders for whatever was needed, then filling the orders at Mrs. Williams'. Liquor could not be bought on the beach, but by driving ashore on my motor-cycle, I was able to get even that commodity. It was soon evident that I was well on my way to making my first million! I added a percentage to the price of every item, charged double for a fifty-pound cake of ice (to allow for melting), and established a set delivery charge. Money kept rolling in —as much as fifteen dollars a day on weekends. By the end of the first summer season, the *Trickey II* and I had accumulated almost three hundred dollars in the coffee can behind the counter in Mrs. Williams' store.

Father and I took full advantage of the sturdiness and sea-worthiness of the *Trickey II*. During the tuna and bluefish season, we ventured forth through Jones Inlet into the open sea, trolling five or so miles off the beach looking for blues, or following the fishing fleet to the Mudhole, off the New Jersey coast, where we'd chum for big tuna.

I remember one trip in particular which was, for us, one of the most enjoyable, but which worried my mother almost half to death. It happened on a Thursday in mid-August. Father and I left the High Hill Beach dock long before daylight. We were loaded for bear. Mother had packed enough lunch for a dozen men; *Trickey II*'s gas tank was filled to capacity, and the motor was tuned to top-notch condition. Our fishing lines, three hundred feet of heavy, tarred hand lines with their piano wire leaders and feather lures, were coiled neatly in butter tubs. The sixteen-foot cypress pole outriggers were lashed securely to the cockpit floor. They extended up and out on a forty-five-degree angle, giving us an awkward, top-heavy appearance, but they were a trolling necessity, so we used them.

We reached Jones Inlet at daybreak. There was hardly a breath of wind; the inlet was calm, except for a gentle ground swell rolling towards us into the bay. We were grateful for the calm; Jones Inlet, with its twisting, ever-changing channel, its treacherous sand bars, its crashing surf in times of storm, was dangerous enough to put fear into the heart of the most expert navigator. Its treachery had brought many a fishing boat to a watery grave.

Father and I were soon in the open sea. We ran our tarred lines over the stern, fastened two to the outriggers by means of the snap clothespins we used for that purpose, and secured the two center lines to cleats on the corners of the aft deck.

Now we were ready. Bring on those blues; those bonito; those tuna!

We trolled hour after hour; first easterly, along the beach, then southward, until we were five or six miles offshore. Father kept scanning the glass-slick waters with his binoculars, looking for diving gulls, leaping schools of bait, anything to indicate a school of blues or tuna was within our reach. We saw nothing to attract our attention. Father thought that the sea was too calm and that the fish were sulking down near the bottom. We trolled steadily until about four o'clock that afternoon, up and down the coast, offshore, inshore, and we still had not had a strike. Around four-thirty, a breeze sprang up from the southwest, kicking up a moderate chop that slapped gently against the *Trickey II* as we moved slowly along at trolling speed. Apparently a few fish decided to venture to the surface, because two of our lines were struck at the same time. The hooked fish stayed deep, fighting all the way in, indicating we'd hooked bonito or small tuna rather than blues, which would have leaped a few times before being landed. Both our lines yielded almost identical school bonito, about three pounds each. We crossed and re-crossed the same area but did not get another strike. It appeared we'd caught the only two fish within miles.

It was about five o'clock then. The wind had risen; the chop had become more severe. There was not another boat in sight.

"Best we be heading home, son," Father announced. "We've got a good five miles to go to the inlet; it'll be another hour and a half before we get home."

I agreed and set our course due west.

We were within two miles of the buoys marking the entrance to the inlet when, directly in front of us, hundreds of terns, or bluefish gulls, as we called them, were skimming the surface of the sea and diving into the schools of bait fish being whipped to a frenzy by the school of feeding bluefish directly below them. I maneuvered our boat around the edge of the school. First one line, then another, then all four lines had been struck. Father and I worked furiously, pulling in our tarred lines hand over hand, flinging the shimmering fish into the cockpit. It was soon evident that the outrigger lines were too much of a nuisance to bother with, so we abandoned them, concentrating our efforts on the nearer center lines. One fish after another was heaved over the stern and into the forward cockpit. We could not get our feather lures more than a dozen feet beyond the stern before a bluefish would strike with all the viciousness for which they are famous. In an hour we had boated about a hundred pounds of school blues, weighing around three pounds apiece. I can say with certainty we'd lost three times that many. A hooked bluefish can throw a lure with ease. Once he has leaped out of water, he gets that little bit of slack line he needs to toss the hook.

"Getting late, son," Father remarked as he straightened up, breathing hard. "We've got to git—right now."

I had to agree, much as I hated to leave that school. Once again I steered for the inlet.

When we reached the bell buoy, the sight we'd seen an hour or so before again confronted us—hundreds of diving, screaming gulls, the water whipped to a froth by thousands of feeding fish. Now, no fisherman worthy of the name could resist a sight like that, and Father and I were no exceptions. We payed out our tarred lines once more, and the slaughter began. By the time either of us took time to straighten up and look around, darkness was almost upon us. The rising wind had kicked up a nasty sea; looking toward the inlet we could see breakers crashing on every bar. The inlet was white water all the way across. We headed our dory in the general direction of that white water. We had no lights of any kind aboard; we'd have to feel our way through that treacherous channel. A swift ebbing tide rushed toward us, pushing the ground swell into foam-flecked mountains of green-black water that bore down upon us. We threaded our way carefully. I steered to port side until I heard the waves crashing on the bar to my left, then I eased to starboard until the awesome sound of rushing white water reached me from the right. The curling combers astern came upon us with lightning speed; often I had to throw the motor into reverse, backing into the oncoming wave, lest it pick us up and throw us headlong onto the ever-present, ever-waiting sandbars. Or, worse yet, lest the onrushing wave carry us forward at such speed that the bow of our boat would be submerged beneath the sea, and we would be swamped in mid-channel.

I guess it took us the better part of an hour to reach the comparatively calm waters of the bay, and it was one of the longest hours I've ever spent. When we could breathe easily again, I could dimly make out my father's face. He was smiling, and I thought I detected admiration in his eyes. During the entire, perilous trip through the inlet, he had stood beside me at the tiller. He'd said not a word, nor had he made any attempt to interfere with my handling of the boat. When it was over, I had the feeling he was proud of the way I'd brought her through.

All he said was, "Guess we've got a pretty good boat, son. Now, let's go home."

We rode the five miles home without incident. I didn't need lights to show me the way. Great South Bay was as familiar to me as my own bedroom.

When we reached the dock at High Hill, we were amazed to see a crowd of people standing there, shouting and waving at us as we glided up to the dock. Mother was there, her eyes red from crying, a tear-drenched handkerchief clutched in her hand. Father and I looked at each other.

"Guess we're gonna catch hell, son," he whispered.

But we didn't; not just then, anyway. Mother was too relieved and happy to see us home safe and sound to even think of scolding us. We learned later that the Coast Guard had sent out two boats to search for us, the State Police were patrolling the beach looking for wreckage, and friends of Mother's and Father's had telephoned for a search plane to leave at daylight. We had passed directly under the eyes of the Coast Guard lookout tower at the inlet and had not been seen. Now I could understand how the rum runners got away with it during the days of prohibition.

"Gee, Mom," I exclaimed, when the plans for our rescue were unfolded, "there wasn't anything to worry about. Besides, look at all the fish we caught!"

It wasn't often that Mother got angry, but when she did, somebody's ears usually got boxed. Mine did this time, though at age sixteen I couldn't figure out what I'd said to deserve it.

There was only one instance I can recall when the *Trickey II* ever let me down. Actually, it wasn't her fault; no motor in the world can run when it's soaking wet. Let me tell you what happened:

My sister's husband was a member of the New York State Police, and during the summer of '34 he was stationed at Fire Island State Park. He and sister Anne invited me and my friend Sam Collins to visit them for a weekend in mid-September.

Sam and I rode the State channel in the *Trickey II* from High Hill Beach to Fire Island, a distance of about twenty miles. In order to get to the island, it was necessary to cross the open bay for the last five miles. We made the trip to Fire Island without incident and spent two days with Anne and Brian, fishing, clamming, swimming, and playing ball on the beach. Sunday afternoon we had to leave; Sam had to be back at his summer job on Monday morning.

Sunday morning dawned rainy, windy, and thoroughly nasty. Our hosts urged us to stay over another day, but I'd made up my mind to get Sam back to his job on time. We left Fire Island about three o'clock that afternoon. The rain had stopped, momentarily, but an east wind, blowing at about forty knots, whipped the open waters of the bay into a white frenzy. We were lucky to have the wind at our backs as we crossed the unprotected five miles; the *Trickey II* scudded across in record time, the whitecaps curling and breaking just inches below her gunwales.

We had just reached the entrance to the State channel,

which ran due west towards home, when a giant wave broke across our stern, filling our little boat with over a foot of water. The spinning flywheel of our motor picked up the water and threw it over the entire ignition system. The motor stopped. Just then the rain started again, this time in a drenching downpour. It was useless to attempt to dry off the motor. Sam went forward to drop the anchor while I held the *Trickey*'s tiller, trying to keep her from broaching broadside against the waves. For the first time since I'd made it a part of the boat's equipment, the twenty-five-pound Navy anchor failed to hold. Sam payed out more than 150 feet of rope, roughly ten times the depth of the channel, but the anchor continued dragging. Sam and I held a council.

"What do you want to do, Sam?" I shouted over the roar of the wind. "Should we try to make it to shore, or would it be better to drift down channel?"

"Seems like the wind's blowing straight down the channel," Sam shouted back. "Suppose we put up the storm hood and let the wind push us home. Maybe the rain'll let up later on so we can get the motor dried out."

I agreed. It was worth a try, anyway. Meanwhile, Sam and I took turns on the hand bilge pump, working furiously to get our boat pumped out before the pouring rain swamped us.

The canvas storm hood, which lay in a semicircle on the forward deck, was quickly raised and secured. The wind filled the hood like a balloon, and we noticed immediately an increase in our forward speed. The rain continued falling in torrents, lashed by the ever-increasing fury of the wind. We were sure the wind's velocity had reached hurricane strength. We learned later that it had.

Darkness fell early that afternoon as we continued to drift westward down the channel. Many times we were sure the howling wind would tear our storm-hood sail to shreds. A heavy ground swell had developed in the channel, its forward movement picking us up on its crest, rushing us downward into its trough, then stopping us in our tracks momentarily as the wave passed beneath our hull. It took both Sam and me on the tiller to hold us on a steady course, always keeping the stern directly in line with the oncoming waves. We had to keep working the bilge pump at intervals, lest the continual downpour fill us to the point where we could no longer maneuver.

We drifted hour after hour. We were soaked to the skin, shivering with cold, and hungry.

"Boy, oh, boy, what I'd give for a nice, hot cup of coffee!"

"Me, too," answered Sam, grinning. "I don't think we'll EVER dry out."

Around midnight, we reached Sanford Island, a bayberry-and-beach-plum-covered blotch of land, which stood at the northeast entrance to Zachs Bay. We were home at last, or nearly so, at least. All we had to do was figure out how an easterly wind could blow us due south to the High Hill Beach dock. So near to home, and yet so far!

Just as we approached Sanford Island, resigned to the fact that we would have to stay there for the rest of the night, the howling gale stopped. So did the rain. We found ourselves in a dead calm, although the channel waves continued pushing us forward. The calm lasted just long enough for us to catch our breaths. We could see the cottages of High Hill outlined against the sky to the south and a little east of where we lay tossing broadside in the ground swell. Suddenly, the storm broke again, its fury as intense as before. But now the howling wind was bearing down upon us from the northwest. Sam and I looked at each other.

"Know what, Sam?" I shouted. "Sometimes I think we got more luck than brains."

"You better believe it, friend," Sam answered. "Let's go home."

We maneuvered the dory's stern to the wind. Once again the storm hood billowed, and we scudded across Zachs Bay toward the High Hill dock.

But when we got there, there was no dock—none that we could see, anyway. The tide had risen well over the top of the bulkhead. I took a wild guess that we were within fifty feet of where the submerged dock should be.

"Drop the bow anchor, Sam," I shouted.

Sam did, then payed out thirty or so feet of line. Luckily, the flukes of the anchor held in the mud, because the stern whipped around, pointing the bow into the wind.

"Put down the storm hood, Sam."

When this was done, Sam again took up his position at the bow anchor line, while I sounded with a push-pole off the stern. It went straight down, hitting nothing. Sam slackened off on the bow line, little by little, as I kept sounding with the pole. Finally, about three feet down, the point of the pole rested solidly. I thumped it and felt wood rather than mud beneath the pole. Sam dropped us back another three feet. The pole still thumped on the solid wood planking of the dock.

"Make her fast right there, Sam," I shouted over the howling wind. "I'm going overboard."

I grabbed up the stern line and jumped into the water. My

feet landed solidly on the invisible dock. I was in water up
to my waist. I groped along carefully in the pitch blackness,
holding on to the stern line. Finally, I brushed against one of
the tie posts which stood at intervals along the outer edge of
the planking. I quickly fastened the stern of the *Trickey II*
securely.

Our biggest problem now was to see to it that our boat
would not be riding on top of the dock when the tide fell. I
moved towards the boat, groping with my feet and hands
until I found the edge of the bulkhead. One more step and
I would have been in twelve feet of water! With my position
to guide him, Sam took up on the anchor line until the stern
of the *Trickey II* was about three feet out from where I
stood. Sam secured the line and moved to the stern.

"Think you can make it, Sam?" I shouted.

"I'd better," Sam shouted back. He leaped, landing on all
fours beside me. We were home at last!

Mother and Father were astounded to see us walk into the
cottage, looking like thoroughly drowned rats. They had
been in bed, asleep, never dreaming that we would attempt
the homeward journey from Fire Island in a hurricane.

Sam and I told them the entire story of our experience
while we sat wrapped in dry blankets at the kitchen table
devouring Mother's flapjacks and coffee. When we'd finished our story and at least two dozen 'jacks, we were hus-
tled off to bed.

After we were snugly beneath the blankets, Father walked
into the bedroom carrying two steaming, half-filled glasses.

"Here, boys," he said, "this'll take the chill out. Can't have
you fellows catching cold, you know."

Sam and I each drank the proffered hot whiskey and sugar. We hardly had time to set the empty glasses down before we were asleep.

That hot drink did the trick, all right. Neither Sam nor I had even so much as a sniffle after our ordeal.

Winters on Long Island were always a terrible bore for me, primarily because they kept me from the beach and fishing, and secondly because they signified the two things I disliked most: going to school and cold, miserable weather. I never enjoyed winter sports particularly; my ankles were too wobbly for ice skating, and the terrain around Hicksville was as flat as a pancake, so there was no tobogganing or sledding to speak of. There were times when the ice in the creeks around Bellmore and Massapequa was solid enough to walk on. Then I'd go with my friends Sam and Eddie to spear eels through the ice. This was good fun for a while, but when my feet got cold and my fingers became numb, I'd had it. I used to say that if the Good Lord wanted us to live in a cold climate, He would have supplied us with fur on our backs.

The advent of spring always brought plans for my return to the bay. It meant scraping *Trickey II*'s bottom, painting her, and oiling and overhauling her motor. Sometimes I think the imagined smell of red copper paint and oakum caulking were the only things that sustained me during those long, cold months of winter.

The spring that *Trickey II* was two years old, Easter vacation came the first week in April. I'd checked and rechecked my tool kit a hundred times the month before. I had new paint brushes, plenty of deck and copper paint,

yacht white for her sides, my caulking irons and mallet—
everything I'd need to put my boat in shape to go overboard
the first of May.

*Trickey II* had spent the winter in dry dock in Carlson's
Boat Yard in Bellmore. On the first day of Easter vacation,
Sam, Eddie, and I were at the yard early, ready to go to
work. Six eager hands made good progress with the scraping and wire brushing. By noon we were well on our way
towards applying the first coat of paint.

It was still pretty cold that early in the spring; the temperatures of both the air and the water were only a few
degrees above freezing. Lunchtime came, and we took
refuge behind a stack of oil drums to get out of the chilling
north wind.

Suddenly, from across the canal, came a hoarse cry for
help. We jumped to our feet and looked in the direction
from which the cry came. We saw an old man standing on a
dock in front of a little grey cottage. He was waving his
arms frantically, repeating his cries for help. Then he pointed
out into the canal. About twenty yards from the dock we
could make out a man's head and, a few feet away, his hat.

Sam, Eddie, and I raced to the head of the canal, then
around on the other side to the dock, where the man stood
waving his arms excitedly. Meanwhile, two employees from
the boat yard had jumped into a rowboat and raced towards
the head bobbing in the water. We watched anxiously as
they towed the body ashore.

My friends and I willingly lent a hand in dragging the
body up on the beach. It was the body of the other man's
brother. They were Polish, both in their sixties, living to-

gether in the little grey cottage. The man on the dock spoke broken English, and that, together with his completely distraught condition, made it difficult for us to understand him. However, we gathered from his story that his brother had deliberately jumped off the dock in an attempted suicide.

We had dragged the body ashore, face down. I suggested we lift the man up on the two-foot-high grassy embankment, with his head slanting downward, so that I might apply artificial respiration until a doctor arrived. Sam and Eddie helped put the body into position. I kneeled above him, straddled his legs, and applied stiff-arm pressure to his rib cage, as I'd learned to do as a boy scout. After a few moments of applied forward pressure, the man's wet body started to slide down the slippery embankment.

"Hey, Sam," I called, "give him a boost back up on the bank, will you? He's slipping away from me."

Sam complied, putting his arms beneath the man's shoulders, giving a boost while I pulled his legs. When the man's body was back up on the bank, Sam removed his arms from beneath the man's shoulders. Sam's sleeves were covered with blood, from his wrists to above his elbows!

We looked at each other. Sam stared stupidly at his jacket sleeves. Eddie took a step backward and stared too.

"Come here, Eddie, give me a hand," I said. "Let's turn him over."

Eddie complied, gingerly. When the man was turned over, his head fell back, revealing a gash that extended across his throat from ear to ear. Both Eddie and I jumped back in horror. One of the men who had effected the rescue with the rowboat took a closer look. Apparently the dead man had slashed both his wrists, cut his throat, then leaped or fallen into the water. His suicide was a very thorough job indeed!

Sam, Eddie, and I took off like scared rabbits. We'd seen enough to last us a long, long time, and at that point I wouldn't have bet a plugged nickel all three of us wouldn't have nightmares for days to come.

The admonitions of both my father and Fred Klemm to be careful on the water and not to take unnecessary chances were printed indelibly in my mind, so what happened to Sam and me one Sunday was, well, not exactly accidental, but definitely unavoidable.

The bluefish had schooled up around the Fire Island light-ship, located about twelve miles south-southeast of Fire Island Inlet. I'd phoned Sam on Friday evening to see if he would be free to go fishing with me that Sunday.

"Why sure, Skip," he told me, eagerly. "Just name the time and place—I'll be there."

True to his word, Sam was waiting for me at the High Hill dock at five o'clock on the morning specified. Our trip, east along the State channel to Fire Island, then south through the inlet, was without incident. It was a beautiful August morning. The wind was calm; the sky, virtually cloudless.

After we'd passed the bell buoy marking the entrance to the inlet, we set about rigging up our tarred trolling lines and the two outriggers.

We hit several blues on the way out, but since the reports of large schools centered around the lightship, we did not linger in the area where we caught the few strays. By the time we reached the lightship, there were at least fifty other boats there ahead of us, all trolling slowly in wide circles. We joined the other fishermen and proceeded to get our share of the three-pound blues.

Sam and I had a wonderful time catching those blues. Actually, only one of us could fish at a time; it took total concentration by the other to steer the *Trickey II* in the unusual amount of traffic all around us. We took turns, usually at about half-hour intervals.

Along about two o'clock, it was my turn at the wheel. I was steering due south; there was a fisherman's skiff trolling parallel with me, about fifty feet off my port side, and another boat about the same distance away on my starboard side, also running parallel. The three boats had been on this southerly course for about twenty minutes.

Several hundred yards off our port bow, a yacht was trolling towards us on a course that would take it directly across our bows. The yacht was about a forty-footer, with its cabin and most of its cockpit glass-enclosed.

I called to my companion, "Hey, Sam, look at that boat off port bow. Ever see so much glass in your life?"

Sam looked up. "Looks like a floating greenhouse, sure 'nuff. He'd better veer off pretty soon. He's fixing to cross in front of us."

"He wouldn't be that stupid, I don't reckon. He'll swing to port and run parallel with us."

Sam scratched his head. "I sure hope so."

We continued holding our course, as did the fishermen on our port and starboard sides. The yacht continued bearing down on us. In no time it was within hailing distance. The two other fishing boat pilots and I shouted at the same time, "Hey! Hey there! Veer off. Hey! Hey there!"

The yacht either did not hear or paid no attention. It continued coming at us. At the last possible moment the boat on our left swung hard to port in order to avoid a collision. The boat on our right swung hard to starboard. It was not possible for me to turn the *Trickey II* in either direction without cutting the trolling lines of one of the other two boats, so I continued to hold my course. The yacht crossed my bow about thirty feet in front of me. I crossed just aft of its stern.

Sam and I both felt the thud as the yacht's trolling lures hit the *Trickey*'s hull. We could see its lines go taut, then go slack. We had cut all six of its lines! The fishermen on the yacht suddenly came alive. We could see them jumping up and down, waving their arms excitedly. The helmsman swung the yacht about, then gunned his motor until he was within hailing distance of us.

"You two kids cut our lines," someone on the yacht shouted. "What do you intend to do about it?"

"Not a thing," I shouted back. "You cut across our bow from port side. We couldn't help what happened. We're sorry about your lines."

"Sorry won't do," came the reply. "You'll pay for them."

"No, we won't."

"You'll pay, or I'll ram you!"

I looked at Sam. He shrugged, telling me more eloquently than words, "It's your boat, Skip. Whatever you do is O.K. by me."

"Go to hell," I shouted brazenly at my adversary. I think I must have pictured myself as David, facing Goliath.

The helmsman circled again, and this time headed directly

for the *Trickey II*. I maintained my course. The yacht struck us a glancing blow on the port side, aft of midships. The *Trickey* tipped to starboard, shipping a few buckets of water over the gunwale, but there was no other damage. The yacht slid past, then drew up alongside, several yards to starboard.

"What about it? You gonna pay for those lines?"

"No!" I shouted back.

One of the crew members on the yacht leaned over the rail and shook his fist at us.

"You're asking for it, sonny," he snarled.

The yacht circled again, then headed directly for us. It hit the *Trickey II* amidship. There was the sound of splintering wood and the tinkle of breaking glass. Our port outrigger had crashed through the foremost of the yacht's cabin windows; the forward momentum of both boats carried the outrigger through every window and window frame on its port side. Both Sam and I were thrown off balance by the impact. By the time we'd gained our footing, both of us were plenty scared.

"That maniac means to sink us, Skip. What'll we do now?" Sam asked.

The yacht lay idle in the water a hundred yards away. It appeared that those aboard were cleaning up the broken glass and splintered wood.

"Let's see how bad we're hurt, Sam." I tried to keep my voice calm.

Examination revealed the top plank on the port side was split for a length of about four feet. The chafing rail on that side was splintered, but the rail had kept us from suffering further damage.

"We were lucky, Sam. We're not hurt bad."

Both of us looked toward the yacht in anticipation of its next attempt to sink us. We were right; the yacht was again under way, starting to make a wide circle toward us.

Meanwhile, about a dozen of the boats that were trolling in the vicinity had witnessed the assault upon us. They moved toward us, forming a circle around the *Trickey II.* The yacht would have to cut through them before it could get at us. Several of the small boat skippers waved or shouted encouragement to us.

The yacht's captain apparently thought better of trying another attack. He realized we had too many friends ready and willing to offer us their protection. The yacht gunned its throttle and sped away. Our little fleet of friends grinned at us and waved, then went back to their fishing.

Sam and I were still pretty badly shaken up. He looked at his watch and said, "It's three-thirty, Skip. Think we've had enough for today?"

"I reckon so, Sam. Let's go home."

We headed for the inlet.

Did you ever attempt to land a lassoed express train from a bobbing cork twenty miles out in the Atlantic? Well, Father and I did, and we landed it, too.

During the months of August and early September, back in the mid-thirties, we made several excursions in the *Trickey II* from Jones Inlet to the Jersey coast, in the vicinity of the Atlantic Highlands. This was considered a long way to go for sport fishing, especially in an eighteen-foot boat, but, believe me, the fun and excitement were well worth it.

Neither Father nor I was ever afraid of the water, but we

had a very healthy respect for it, especially the unpredictable, precarious Atlantic Ocean. Then, too, Father never understood or appreciated the workings of a gasoline motor; consequently, he trusted the *Trickey II*'s Model A Ford conversion about as far as he could throw it. Thus, on each occasion that we planned a tuna fishing expedition to the Jersey coast, Father would drive over to the charter boat dock in Freeport and advise the captains with whom we were acquainted that we'd meet them "in the Mudhole" the following day. They assured Father that they would keep an eye out for us. This meant, of course, that in case of a sudden squall or a motor breakdown, we would have a dozen friends there to see to our safety.

On several of our trips, we spent the day trolling the "acid water" around Ambrose lightship. The acid water is a phenomenon which occurs in the tidal stream that empties from New York Harbor into the Atlantic. This tidal stream is a muddy brown and contains floating refuse from the sewers of the city. The acid water is a natural feeding ground for school tuna, and fish weighing from fifteen to thirty pounds are caught by trolling feather lures or silver spoons.

A tuna hits hard. His initial, smashing jolt will send shock waves from your fingertips to your shoulder, and this is only the beginning. We trolled tarred lines in those days, and many times our hands were burnt to blisters by the lightning speed with which a thirty-pound tuna ripped off line in his first rush for the bottom. A tuna will always dive deep when he feels the bite of the hook; I have never seen one break water like a sailfish or bluefish.

Usually, Father and I would cut *Trickey*'s motor when

we'd hooked a big one. It was more fun fighting him from a standstill than it was "horsing him in" with a moving boat to stack the odds in our favor. Tuna are trolled at a much faster rate of speed than one trolls for bluefish. The lure is trolled close to the stern of the boat; whereas blues are trolled from 150 to 200 feet back. I understand it is the spinning propeller and white wake that entice tuna to come up from the depths to investigate.

Our charter boat friends, as well as the newspaper fishing columns, kept us informed as to when giant tuna were being taken from the Mudhole. We waited anxiously for those first reports, hoping that when the tuna were there, the weather would be favorable enough for us to set a course for the New Jersey coast.

Finally, in late August, we got word that practically every charter boat skipper had brought in a good catch. The fish were running from sixty to a hundred and fifty pounds, and there seemed to be plenty of them.

I think Father was as excited as I when we made preparations for the trip. We were going on Sunday, so the Saturday evening before, I drove to Freeport to tell our friends to expect to see us the next day, and also to load up with chum and bait. I bought two ten-gallon garbage cans filled with ground-up moss bunker from the Freeport Fish Co. for chum and twenty-odd pounds of whole bunker for bait. I also borrowed a pair of heavy fishing rods, equipped with five-hundred-yard star-drag reels from our friend Captain Lewis, who lent them to us gladly, since he did not have a charter scheduled for the following day. We were going after the big ones with rod and reel this time. Tar lines were far too dangerous to handle on fish the size we were after.

Sunday dawned a perfect day. By sunrise we were just south of the Jones Inlet whistling buoy, in the company of two charter fishing boats, all heading south-southwest to the Mudhole. Even *Trickey II* seemed infected with our excitement. She purred like a kitten, riding the long, rolling ground swell like a chip on a millstream.

We reached the Mudhole, which lies south-southeast of Ambrose lightship, about three hours out of Jones Inlet. The other fishing boats dropped their anchors, and we did likewise, only to find that our anchor rope was not long enough to reach bottom. We had not prepared for that possibility; it had never occurred to us that the Mudhole was that deep.

"What'll we do now, Dad?" I inquired. "Shall we drift?"

"Can't do that, son. Too many boats fishing all around us. We'd drift through their chum slicks. Let's head for that lobster pot marker over there."

A few hundred yards away I saw what Father meant. A bamboo pole, topped by a black and white flag, swayed gently in the ground swell. The pole marked the location of a lobsterman's trap. It was well anchored and appeared to be the answer to our problem. We soon secured our bow line to it.

It took only a short time for us to rig our lines. It was a simple rig, consisting of a swivel, ten feet of piano wire, and a 12/0 hook. We baited with whole bunker, then paid out about fifty feet of line. We watched the bait drift back slowly with the tide.

Using a sugar scoop we'd brought along for the purpose, I shoveled up a scoopful of the ground bunker from one of the garbage cans and spattered it astern. It drifted in the direction of our bait. I followed this procedure at about five-minute intervals.

Suddenly, as I watched a glob of chum sink slowly, there was a flash of blue lightning through the water. The chum disappeared!

"Look, Dad," I cried excitedly. "Watch this!"

I threw another glob of chum over the stern. Again that streak of silver-blue, and again the chum disappeared.

"That's tuna, my boy," Father said, almost in awe, "darn big tuna!"

I worked my line frantically, reeling in, letting out, jerking the line to simulate the action of a live bait. Father did the same to his line. Nothing happened! I continued chumming; the tuna continued gobbling up the chum, but for some unknown reason, they refused to take our bait.

Two hours passed, and we were thoroughly exasperated. We were down to our last half can of chum and still had not had a strike.

We had brought along one other piece of fishing equipment which I've forgotten to mention. Tucked safely in Father's back pocket were a half-dozen packages of lady's hairnets. Father took one now and filled it with a glob of chum. He removed the whole bunker from his hook and substituted the hairnet, twisting and weaving the hook into the fine strands. He again dropped his line over the stern and allowed the glob to drift back with the tide. Nothing! I threw over another scoop of chum. It disappeared almost instantly.

"Dad," I said, "I think I have an idea. Reel in your line; I'd like to try something."

Father said nothing, but did as I asked.

"Now then," I directed, "give me some slack."

I coiled about twenty feet of his line at my feet, then held the piano wire leader just above the hairnet. With my right hand, I took up another scoop of chum. Then, as I threw it overboard, I tossed the hairnet-covered hook into the middle of the chum, paying out Father's line slowly so that the bait drifted out with the chum.

I saw the silver-blue flash at the same moment a terrific jolt hit my left arm, nearly pulling it from its socket. I cried out, then let go the line. I did not even see the coil of line disappear, it happened so fast. Almost at the same instant, Father also let out a yell and both his arms snapped taut as he gripped the rod desperately to keep it from being pulled from his hands. The reel screamed in protest as yard after precious yard of line was torn from it. That first rush was for almost three hundred yards, and, from all appearances, the fish had just begun to fight.

"Let go the bow line, son," Father panted. "We're in for a fight. Don't want to upset that lobster pot down there."

When we were adrift, the *Trickey II* started moving slowly in the direction the fish was going. Suddenly, the forward movement stopped while the tuna rested momentarily, gathering strength.

Slowly Father pumped the rod, reeling as he did so, gaining line yard by yard and foot by foot. The tuna allowed him to regain about half the yardage lost on that first run; then, with its strength renewed, the fish started a second run, even more devastating than the first. Father's face and body poured perspiration as he leaned back against the force of the big fish. I used my handkerchief to wipe the perspiration from his eyes, and, at the same time, poured a bucket of sea water over the now-smoking reel. Father was seated on the engine hatch, his feet braced against the stern locker. I could see his arm and shoulder muscles quiver as he matched every ounce of his strength against his worthy opponent.

The fight lasted over an hour, during which time the *Trickey II* was towed around and around in hundred-yard-wide circles by the seemingly tireless monster. Once, during the battle, I asked Father if he wanted me to take the rod awhile. He looked up at me and grinned.

"Hell, no, son," he panted, "I'm having too much fun to quit now!"

Finally, we had the fish straight down, alongside the boat. Slowly, ever so slowly, Father's ebbing strength retrieved the last hundred yards of line. I looked over the side and could see the fish clearly, though it was still fifty feet down. It looked as long as the *Trickey II*! Its head was still pointed towards the bottom, but its fighting strength was almost gone.

"Get the gaff, son," Father said.

I grasped the handle of the six-foot gaff firmly in my left hand. Now I must judge the distance between me and the fish. The depth was deceiving—a lunge and miss might well cause us to lose him.

"Steady, boy," Father admonished as he continued reeling.

The fish was just below the surface now. I grabbed the wire leader in my gloved right hand and jerked the gaff hook through the expanded gills of the tuna. It took all our strength to lift the shuddering fish into the boat.

"Wow!" I shouted. "What a monster!"

Father grinned, too exhausted to give vent to the pleasure I knew he felt. Both of us just sat there on the engine hatch looking at our prize. Its body was as long as the boat's forward cockpit.

"How much do you figure it weighs, Dad?"

"A hundred and fifty easy," he guessed.

It was a pretty good guess, at that. The fish weighed in at one hundred and fifty-two pounds.

We started for home. It was getting late, we had a long way to go, and besides—what would we ever do with another monster that size?

It will not be easy for me to tell you this next story. Even though it happened over thirty years ago, it is still very much alive in my memory, and I guess it always will be. It is the story of how I lost the *Trickey II*.

If she had been lost in a storm or sunk on a reef in the inlet, perhaps the telling would not be so painful. It would have been an acceptable, even a natural fate for a boat that had served me well for six wonderful years. When I lost her, I believe I lost a part of me, too.

In the winter of '38, I left college and got married. This was contrary to my father's wishes, and he told me so in no uncertain terms. I was able to get a job with an engineering firm on Long Island, which paid me the enormous sum of twelve dollars a week. I should have realized it would not be long before I would have financial difficulties; it took three weeks' salary to pay the rent on our apartment over the cigar store in Hicksville.

The following year, our difficulties were compounded when we discovered we were going to become parents sometime in the early spring.

Jobs were hard to come by in 1939. A salary of even twenty-five dollars a week was considered a modest, though satisfactory income.

My luck had seemingly run out, and, with the baby coming, I needed money desperately. With my wife urging and prodding, I finally agreed to swallow my pride and go to Father for help. I arrived at my parents' house just as he and Mother were finishing supper. The maid had just served the coffee.

"Dad," I said bluntly, "I need your help."

"Oh?" he said, setting down his cup. "What is it you want?" The tone of his voice was wary, even a little hostile, I noticed, but I tried to ignore it.

"I need to borrow a hundred dollars; with the baby coming and all—" My voice trailed away. I looked into his eyes, but there was no warmth in them.

"I suppose you do," he replied. "What do you have to put up for collateral?"

"Collateral?" I was shocked. "You know I don't have anything, only my job. I don't have any collateral."

"You own a boat." Father's voice was stern.

"Sure I do—I own the *Trickey II*. O.K., I'll put up my boat against a hundred-dollar loan. I'll pay it back—just wait and see." My voice showed my relief.

"I'm afraid that won't do, son. I really don't expect you'll ever be in a position to pay it back. I'll tell you what I'll do, though. I'll buy the *Trickey II* from you for the hundred dollars. I'm sure your brother would like to have it."

I know I turned as white as the dining room tablecloth. Did I hear correctly? Would he really do this to me? I searched his face, his eyes, for some sign of a twinkle, a little twitch of a smile that would show me he was just kidding. There was no twinkle, only determination. There was no smile, only stern reproach. I looked across the table at my mother. She smiled weakly, and I thought I saw mist in her eyes. She said nothing. I thought then of my wife Evelyn, waiting at home, waiting for the money. I thought, too, of the hours of verbal haranguing I was in for if I failed to bring it.

When I could trust myself to speak again, I asked, "Dad, are you sure you couldn't just lend me the money?"

"It wouldn't be good business. I'll either buy the boat outright, or you'll have to get along without the money."

I felt the tears in my eyes, and I turned away, ashamed.

"O.K., Dad." I know my voice shook. "I'll bring over the *Trickey*'s papers tomorrow."

Dad said nothing. He reached into his side pocket, took out a roll of bills, and peeled off five twenties from the outside of the roll. He handed me the money.

"Thank you," I murmured. "Thank you very much. I hope brother Henry likes your present."

I left by the back door. I don't believe I ever felt as alone as I did at that moment.

I imagine my kid brother enjoyed owning the *Trickey II*. I never really knew because I was never invited aboard her by her new owner. Eventually, he sold her. To brother Henry, the *Trickey II* was just a boat; to me, it was a dear friend.

# 3 ~ A Mate for Dorothy

THE ADVENT of spring that first year with my wife Evelyn rekindled the usual nostalgic longings within me to return to salt water. I'd given up my job at the engineering company because, although I got a raise from thirty to thirty-five cents an hour, my work week was cut to three days because of lack of contracts. I spent the winter shoveling coal for a local fuel company for fifty cents an hour. This job, of course, petered out with the coming of spring.

I looked forward, eagerly, to the return of the charter boat fleet from their winter quarters in Florida. I thought perhaps, with their return to the Freeport docks, there would be a mate's job available to me.

I believe it was in early May when my vigil was rewarded by the sight of fifteen or twenty boats rocking gently in their usual berths along Freeport's municipal docks. Among them was the *Spindrift*, captained by my friend Cy Lewis. I lost no time in boarding the *Spindrift* to renew old acquaintances and to seek Captain Lewis's help. When I inquired about a job, my friend was sympathetic and understanding.

"I've still got Tommy workin' for me, kid. If I didn't, I'd sure be glad to give you a job."

"Do you happen to know of any other boat that needs a mate?"

"Let's see now." Captain Lewis removed his battered cap and ran his fingers through his heavy thatch of steel-grey hair. "Maybe I do, at that. I know Captain McFarland on the *Dorothy K* was lookin' for a mate just yesterday. Let me give him a call."

Captain Lewis switched on his ship's short-wave radio: "WSPD *Spindrift*, callin' *Dorothy K*. WSPD *Spindrift*, callin' *Dorothy K*."

Captain Lewis's voice was soft, a Southern drawl giving it a pleasant, musical sound. There was no answer to the call, so it was repeated several times. Finally an answer crackled through the receiver.

"WDWK *Dorothy K* back to *Spindrift*. Come in, Cy."

"*Spindrift* to *Dorothy K*. Hi, Mac. What's doin' over there on First Street?"

"Nothing much, Cy," Mac replied. "Just setting up my new outriggers. I was out on deck; that's why it took me awhile to answer. What can I do for you?"

"Have you found a mate yet?"

"No, I haven't, Cy. Know of anyone looking for a job?" Mac's voice was crisp, with a trace of New England Yankee rather than the Southern accent of so many of the other charter boat captains.

"I've got a young fella here with me now; he's a good boy around boats—known him and his family for years. He's lookin' for a job with the fleet."

"That's fine, Cy. Send him around. WDWK *Dorothy K* off with the *Spindrift*."

I thanked Captain Lewis, then lost no time driving around to where the *Dorothy K* was berthed on First Street.

She was a beautiful boat—a forty-foot Wheeler, powered by twin Chrysler Imperial motors. Her sleek hull was white; above deck she was polished mahogany and shining brass. Gold letters across her stern identified her: "*Dorothy K*—Freeport, N.Y."

When I stepped aboard, I saw the four mahogany fishing chairs fastened by chrome stanchions to the deck of the stern cockpit. Behind them was a lounge cabin, outfitted with cushioned divans which could be converted into upper and lower berths. A drop-leaf table was secured in the middle of the cabin between the two divans. Forward were the wheel, dashboard, and motor controls. A pilot's chair was mounted high enough to give a clear view through the broad expanse of tinted windshield. Directly above the pilot's controls, on the roof of the cabin, was the flying bridge, with its canvas, semicircular apron fastened to chrome stanchions and railing. The flying bridge contained a steering wheel, twin throttles and clutch controls, a box compass, and twin tachometers.

I stepped into the lounge cabin. A flight of three steps led down into a fully equipped galley; forward of the galley was the Master's cabin, containing two berths, built-in storage cabinets, and a head. A short ladder led from the Master's cabin up through a hatch to the forward deck.

Returning to the stern cockpit, I noticed the outriggers extending straight up about midships alongside the lounge cabin. They were about twenty-five feet high, made of bamboo and painted white. Halyards passed through a pully at the tips of the outriggers. Fastened to the halyards were spring-type clothespins.

My close examination of the *Dorothy K* was interrupted by the approach of a man wearing a tan yachting cap with ensignia identifying him as a ship's captain. When he stepped aboard, I introduced myself.

"Glad to have you aboard," he said, smiling. "I'm Captain McFarland, but just call me Mac." We shook hands.

Captain Mac was shorter than I'd expected, though why I should have visualized him as being tall I really don't know. He was about five feet six, I'd say, ruddy faced, sandy haired. In his chino shirt and pants and captain's cap, he gave the impression of having a military background. Mac's eyes were light blue; the sun and wind lines around his eyes made him appear to be perpetually squinting. His voice was crisp, authoritative, with that hint of New England Yankee twang that had been evident over the radio.

Captain Mac proceeded to show me around the *Dorothy K.* It was then I noticed that he walked with a decided limp in his left leg. That leg was shorter than the right one, and he used it stiff-legged.

When our tour of inspection was over, Mac indicated one of the fishing chairs in the stern cockpit. I took the chair indicated, while he occupied the other. He sat with his "game" leg extended out stiffly in front of him.

"So you want to mate for me," he said abruptly. "Know anything about fishing?"

I told him of the years spent on High Hill Beach, of the *Trickey II* and our trips offshore. I explained I'd been handling boats since boyhood.

"Not meaning to brag, Skipper," I concluded, "but I reckon I've squeezed more salt water out of my socks than a lot of folks my age have seen in their lifetime."

Captain Mac smiled. "I guess I can use you. The pay is three dollars a day plus half the tips, when we sail. If we don't have a charter you don't get paid, but I expect you here to clean up, polish brass, and generally make yourself useful. Is that understood?"

"Yes, it is, Captain. When do I start?"

"Let's see—today's Wednesday. We have a charter Friday, another on Saturday, and the boss will want to go out on Sunday. Suppose you be here tomorrow morning around seven, and you can spend the day cleaning up."

I assured him eagerly that I'd be there in the morning. We shook hands, and I thanked him for taking me on. I drove back to Queens County to my mother-in-law's home, where Evelyn and I were living, since I'd been earning only meager salaries of late. I drove with my head in the clouds, my feet walking on air. At last I'd gotten the kind of job I'd dreamed of, my first real chance at being a commercial fisherman.

The following morning I took Evelyn with me to Freeport. I wanted her to see the *Dorothy K* and also to spend the day looking for a furnished room near the waterfront. I did not relish the idea of driving from Queens County to Freeport at four in the morning in order to be ready to sail at five.

By the time I'd finished my deck swabbing, brass polishing, and general cleaning chores that first day, Evelyn had found a large, sunny, one-room efficiency apartment in Mrs. Frisby's old-fashioned rooming house on Grove Street, just a few blocks from the dock. We paid the weekly rent of five dollars in advance.

The charter parties we accommodated that first Friday and Saturday were an entirely new experience for me and were great fun. I was a little nervous at first, not knowing just what was expected of me, but I handled the lines to everyone's satisfaction, ran the boat from the flying bridge for hours at a time while we trolled slowly for blues and bonito, and made myself as useful to Captain Mac as I could. He did not comment one way or the other as to my efficiency; suffice it to say, I didn't get fired.

Sunday morning I met Mr. and Mrs. Kay, the owners of the *Dorothy K*. After they had stepped aboard and I had their gear safely stowed below, Mr. Kay addressed me directly:

"Now, Mate, if you and I are to get along, there's one thing you must learn to do the minute I step aboard. You are to hand both me and Mrs. Kay a whiskey sour. I don't mean any whiskey sour. I mean one freshly made, with fresh squeezed lemons, just enough, but not too much powdered sugar, and a double shot of whiskey. Don't ever forget that— a double shot of whiskey. I don't want you serving me lemonade; I want a whiskey sour. And remember this, too. When our glasses are empty, I expect you to be standing there with refills. Not a half hour later; right then and there. Understand?"

I said that I did. Apparently, Captain Mac knew the boss man pretty well, because he handed both Mr. and Mrs. Kay a filled glass as soon as they were settled in the lounge.

At the first opportunity after we'd cast off, I approached the skipper.

"Hey, Mac," I whispered, "'what's a whiskey sour?'"

He just looked at me in amazement.

Mrs. Kay, first name Dorothy, of course, was a tall, willowy, sexy-looking blonde, much more friendly than her husband. It amazed me that she could match Mr. Kay drink for drink, from five in the morning until they left the boat twelve hours later, and not show the first sign of inebriation. I wish I could say the same for Mr. Kay.

Both Mr. and Mrs. Kay were good sailors. Many times during that summer we had them aboard in pretty nasty weather, but neither of them ever became ill. Perhaps the whiskey they consumed acted as a soothing syrup for their stomachs.

Speaking of getting seasick, it's amazing the various cures and remedies that were expounded to me by various people we had aboard the *Dorothy K* that summer. Some refused to eat anything all day for fear they'd end up "tossing their cookies" over the rail. Others ate like gluttons, theorizing that a full stomach is a contented, thus quiet, stomach. The virtues of a variety of patent medicines were expounded, running the gamut from Mother Sills Seasick Remedy to Alka-Seltzer. Probably the strangest remedy of all was the one invented by a doctor who fished with us. He had a zinc plate fitted in the bottom of each shoe. Wires ran from one plate, up his pant leg, beneath his shirt, across his shoulders, then down his leg to the other plate. The doctor theorized he had set up a galvanic action through his body which would stabilize his equilibrium. Loss of equilibrium, he said, is the cause of *mal de mer*. I do believe if we had ever been caught at sea in a severe thunderstorm, the good doctor would have lit up like a Christmas tree.

I always dreaded to see children brought aboard the *Dorothy K* by their parents for a day's fishing trip. Not that I had an aversion towards kids; they just didn't belong on a deep sea fishing boat. It was almost impossible to keep them seated in one place for more than ten minutes at a time; they usually chose to roam all over the unfamiliar environment, from flying bridge to fo'cas'le. I felt it was my duty as mate to keep track of them while their parents fished. Sometimes this was virtually an impossible responsibility.

There is something about the internal organs of little kids that makes them—and I mean each and every one of them—susceptible to seasickness.

"Mommy, I don't feel so good!" was an altogether too familiar complaint which I came to expect.

"Go with the mate, dear; he'll take care of you. Mother's fishing."

I'd lead the poor kid to the lounge cabin, see that he was stretched out on the divan, then proceed to surround the bed with buckets, pots, pans—anything that looked like a receptacle.

"Now, if you feel like throwing up, be sure you lean way out of the bunk, with your head over a bucket," I admonished.

"O.K.," came the weak reply.

Invariably, I heard the sound of retching before I'd reached the stern cockpit. I didn't have to turn around; I knew what had happened. The stupid kid had upchucked all over the pillow, all over the bulkhead, all over the upholstered divan—every place but in a bucket. When kids were aboard, I never ate much. They had a tendency to take away my appetite.

The *Dorothy K* kept pretty busy that summer. We must have averaged five charters a week. I received my daily pay of three dollars for each charter, plus an average of two-fifty a day as my half of the tip the party left us. Five-fifty a day for five days—not bad—and a darn sight better than shoveling coal for twenty dollars a week!

Fishing was good that year. We hit blues and bonito during the early part of the season, school tuna and an occasional giant tuna from the Mudhole during the early fall. I don't recall a single trip when we came in with an empty fish box. Captain MacFarland was a good fisherman and a good skipper. He worked hard to find fish for his charter parties.

Toward the end of September, Mac informed me that we had a weekend charter booked for a trip to Brielle, New Jersey. We would leave Friday evening and return sometime Sunday. That Friday we also had a daytime fishing party scheduled. When we returned to our dock on Friday afternoon, our weekend guests were already waiting for us. We unloaded our daytime fishermen, then proceeded to load on our second party—six salesmen from a New York liquor distribution company. I don't believe I have ever seen such a tremendous amount of food and liquor brought aboard a fishing boat. There was case after case of gin, whiskey, beer, and all the makings for mixed drinks. So much, in fact, that we had to open the deck hatches in order to stow some of the cases in the hold. To feed eight people for two days and two nights they had two whole baked hams, three roast turkeys, three roast chickens, two large platters of sandwiches, potato salad, six loaves of bread, butter, and, well, you name it, these dudes brought it. If they had done nothing but eat and drink during the entire trip, they'd have only put a dent in that much food.

We made the trip to Brielle without incident. We sailed in total darkness most of the way; but, as I've said, Captain Mac was a good skipper, and he hit Brielle Inlet right on the nose. We tied up at the Brielle Yacht Club dock at about midnight. During the entire trip the party was a jolly bunch. They sat in the lounge drinking and telling stories. By the time we reached Brielle none of them were "feeling any pain."

Captain Mac checked our mooring lines, then told me, "I'm going ashore with the party. You stay aboard and look after things. When you get tired, crawl into one of the lounge bunks. We won't be gone long."

"O.K., Skipper," I replied, "have fun. See you later."

I guess it was about three in the morning when I was awakened by our returning guests. They were a noisy bunch, singing, shouting, and laughing as they staggered down the dock towards the *Dorothy K.* Our captain was laughing and singing as loudly as the rest. I lay in my bunk, sleepy-eyed, not wanting to be routed out by this bunch of happy drunks. I heard Mac say:

"Now wait up, you guys. You can't make it aboard 'til I pull in the stern. Better let me go first."

I felt the boat being pulled slowly astern. The spring lines stretched taut as did the bridled bow lines, but the stern was still about four feet from the dock. Mac let go the line he was pulling and made a leap for the aft deck. That time his judgment of distance was terrible. He missed the deck, and a loud KERSPLASH evidenced the fact that he was now floundering around somewhere between the boat and the dock. The party of salesmen roared with laughter.

"Should have made it in two, Mac," one of them shouted as he peered over the edge. "Should have made it in two!"

I leaped from my bunk and ran out on deck in my underpants. I secured our boarding ladder over the side at the stern, then directed Mac to it. He finally pulled himself aboard, laughing, spitting, sputtering, a lot wetter and a lot more sober than when he fell in.

Saturday morning dawned miserable, wet and windy. We ventured through Brielle Inlet for a day's fishing, but after being buffeted about for a few hours, the party decided to give up fishing in favor of returning to the protected waters of the bay. I don't believe they were too interested in fishing anyway. They seemed to be having a wonderful time playing cards, eating, and (mostly) drinking. I spent a lazy day, too, cleaning up a bit and catching up on the sleep I hadn't gotten the night before.

Sunday morning was just as bad, weatherwise, as Saturday, perhaps even worse. Brielle Inlet was white water all the way across; the ground swell had built up considerably after twenty-four hours of steady gale-force winds. Captain Mac did not suggest to the party that we try going out fishing. It was obvious how uncomfortable it would be out there.

Shortly after noon it was decided that we would head back to Freeport. The wind was still blowing hard from the east; the morning drizzle increased to a steady, cold rain.

We cleared Brielle Inlet, then set our course north-northeast. The wind, chop, and heavy ground swell were on our starboard quarter, pitching and tossing us around like a matchstick. A particularly heavy, white-crested swell hit us broadside, sending glasses, dishes, and salesmen crashing to the floor. I stood silently next to Mac, awaiting orders.

"This rain has my windshield so fogged up I can't see," he said. "Go topside and take the wheel. Follow our course north-northeast."

I buttoned up my oilskins, pulled my hat down hard on my head, then made my way topside, holding on for dear life as the *Dorothy K* rolled and wallowed in the heavy sea.

I jiggled the wheel to let Mac know I had control from the flying bridge. I took my seat at the wheel, holding myself as steady as I could by wrapping my legs around the chrome stanchions that supported the bridge. The *Dorothy K* lumbered on at quarter throttle. She yawed from port to starboard; occasionally a wave would be so high that, in its trough, our outriggers lay flat against the crest of the giant wave that followed. I'll admit the thought occurred to me that she might yaw once too often and be unable to right herself again. My course was, of necessity, erratic. Several times I swung sharply to starboard to take a particularly heavy swell head-on instead of risking a broadside encounter. Several hours went by. My arms ached from fighting the wheel; my body was a hundred bruises from being buffeted against the guardrails. Suddenly there came a heavy clap of thunder, followed by several more. Sharp, vivid lightning streaked across the sky.

"That's all we need," I grumbled aloud, thoroughly disgusted, "a thunderstorm in the middle of this mess!"

The thought had scarcely crossed my mind when a blinding flash of lightning and a ball of fire hit the water a few yards in front of the boat. I watched, fascinated, as the fiery ball seemed to skip over the water towards me.

What happened next is an indistinct blur in my memory, but as nearly as I can figure it out, the ball of lightning hit our chrome stem piece, traveled up and across the forward deck, then entered the chrome railing and stanchions of the flying bridge. With my legs wrapped tightly around those stanchions, it's no wonder I felt as though someone had hit me hard behind the ear with a belaying pin. The shock knocked me over backward, and the next thing I knew, I'd tumbled off the cabin roof and was flat on my back on the stern cockpit floor. I've often wondered what would have happened if the boat had yawed suddenly, just as I was somersaulting off the roof. Probably I would have ended up as shark bait.

The fall stunned me, but no bones were broken, and I was soon on my feet again. Captain Mac looked at me quizzically.

"You O.K.?"

"Good as new—almost," I answered with what I thought was a reassuring smile, but which turned out to be a sickly grin. "I'm O.K., honest. Want me to go back topside?"

"Sure you don't mind?" Mac asked.

"Don't mind at all. Give me a minute to get up there. I'll take her to the bell buoy; you'd better take her through the inlet."

"That'll be about right," Mac replied. "I'll join you up there later."

I returned to the flying bridge. As we approached the Long Island coast, the shallower water was less bumpy. At about the time I sighted the whistling buoy marking the entrance to Jones Inlet, Captain Mac joined me on the bridge. He left the wheel in my hands; his presence reassured me that I could bring us through without difficulty.

When we left our party at the dock that evening, I was surprised and delighted when one of them handed me a ten-dollar bill.

"I got the feelin' you'll make a pretty good skipper some-day, kid," he said, patting me on the back. "Good luck to you—and thanks."

After they had left, I attempted to give half the money to Mac.

"That's all yours, kid," he said, firmly. "I got one just like it. Before I forget it, here's your three days' pay—and an extra five. I'd say you earned it."

I guess I was grinning from ear to ear as I pocketed the money.

"Oh, another thing," Mac added. "We've got so damn much food left over I'll never use it in a hundred years. When you go home, take all you can carry. Just help yourself."

I did, and Evelyn and I ate baked ham, chicken, turkey, and all the trimmings for a week. I didn't ask Mac about the leftover liquor. It was none of my business.

We continued running charters three or four days a week until about mid-October. The weather turned pretty cool then, which meant that both blues and tuna left our area until the next summer. I knew the *Dorothy K* would be leaving for Florida by the end of October. I wanted to go along so I could continue working for Captain Mac, but it just wasn't possible. Evelyn was expecting and wanted to be near her family when her baby was due to arrive. Then, too, I would not be earning any money until we started taking out parties in Florida. Usually, it was after Christmas be-fore the season started there.

I said good-bye to Mac with deep regret.

# 4 ~ I Learn about Shrimpers–the Hard Way

FOR THE NEXT TEN YEARS I was, of necessity, a dry-land sailor. I say "of necessity" because I was too busy raising a family of four kids and providing a home for them and Evelyn to spend time dreaming of the vagabond life of a fisherman. Oh, I dreamed, all right, but did not even attempt to make those dreams come true. But Fate has a way of changing things, especially when she has a willing accomplice such as I.

Each year, in the spring, I'd find myself being drawn by the sights, smells, and sounds of the waterfront. Invariably, I'd end up in some bar in South Freeport, drinking beer and swapping yarns with the commercial fishermen who would stop in for a few beers before supper. They would troop in, singly or in groups, bringing with them the smell of fish, tar, and diesel oil, their boots and mackinaws salt-stained, still moist with flying spray. I knew most of them by name; they knew me as the little guy who was one of them in his heart, if not in actuality.

One afternoon in early April, 1949, I was sitting alone in the Anchor Bar waiting for some of the boys to show up for their usual beers and conversation. A plain-looking little woman, whom I judged to be in her mid-fifties, took the stool next to me and ordered a beer. I guess it was only natural that we'd strike up a conversation, since we were the only two customers in the bar that early in the afternoon.

"Howdy, sonny," she said, pleasantly. "Nice day, ain't it?"

I agreed that it was.

"I've seen you in here a couple times before. You from around here?" she inquired, sipping her brew politely.

"Not far from here," I told her. "I just like the Anchor. I meet a lot of the fishermen here."

"You ain't a fisherman," she said, looking me over from head to toe. "No offense, sonny; you ain't got the hands nor the clothes to be a fisherman. Now take my husband Poop. He's built slight like you, but he's a sight rougher lookin'— burnt almost black he is—and his hands is one big, horny callus. Why, if he wore them clothes you got on, that neck-tie and all, he'd think he was goin' to a funeral—his own, most likely. No offense, sonny."

I assured her there was no offense taken.

"You say your husband—what did you say his name was?"

"Poop," she answered proudly, "Poop Deck Charlie Sim-mons is his name. I call him Poop for short."

"I'm pleased to meet you, Mrs. Simmons." I told her my name.

"Glad to meetcha," she murmured, shaking my hand. "Want another beer?"

"Let's both have another—my treat." She seemed satisfied to let me do the buying.

"Tell me about your husband, Mrs. Simmons. Is he fishing now?"

"Yeah, old Poop is fishin' all right. Works on a shrimper down in South Carolina. He left for there a week ago—the season ain't really started yet. This is his third year with the fleet. Last year he did well, real well. Made a pile o' money. A lot more'n he ever made around here, I can tell you. This year they promised to give him his own boat. Cap'n Poop! Imagine that!"

My imagination had already run far ahead of the little old lady. I could just see those beautiful, big trawlers making their way through some tropical inlet to the open sea. I longed to be a part of that carefree life; I know the longing showed in my voice when I spoke.

"Gee, Mrs. Simmons, do you think Poop might need a mate?"

"Striker, sonny. On shrimpers they call the deck hand a striker. Might be he could use you, 'specially since you're from around here and all. Tell you what—I'll give you the name and address of the fleet captain. He does all the hirin'. He's from Long Island, too. Maybe he'll take you on, if you decide to go down there. Tell him Cactus sent you. That's me, Cactus Simmons."

I gave Mrs. Simmons a blank card and my pen. She wrote:

Captain John Harvey
c/o Post Office
Beaufort, South Carolina

I left the Anchor Bar a short while later, my head in the clouds. I drove directly home, anxious to tell Evelyn all about my conversation with the lady with the unlikely name of Cactus.

"You know," she said after hearing my story, "maybe it would be good for all of us to get away from Long Island for a while. I know how you hate the cold weather, and you like any kind of fishing—" She hesitated a moment. "If it's what you want, I say let's go."

I could have hugged her. In fact, I did, as I recall.

I lost no time in writing to Captain Harvey in Beaufort, hoping against hope that he did not have a full crew and would accept me sight unseen. Meanwhile, I got road maps from gas stations and looked up Beaufort in the Atlas, learning as much as I could about the unfamiliar part of the country in which I was anxious to seek my fortune.

I got my reply from Captain Harvey in about ten days. He wrote that he would be glad to have me come down, adding that I'd probably feel very much at home with all the other Long Islanders he had working on his shrimpers.

The letter caused a flurry of activity, the likes of which are seldom seen. Evelyn and I talked of little else, and somehow we completed the myriad little details and chores prior to the first of May, the day we'd chosen for our departure. A few days before we planned to leave, I visited Father and Mother and told them of our plans.

"Do you mean to tell me you're going to be fool enough to pack up a wife and four kids and take them on a wild goose chase, just on the strength of a barroom conversation?" Father was incredulous and very, very angry.

"It's what I want to do, Dad," I replied, defensively. "I want to be a commercial fisherman. I know I'll make out all right."

"Oh, is that so?" Father's voice was filled with disdain. "Every commercial fisherman I ever knew ended up with a wet butt and a hungry gut—nothing else. And that's what you will bring to yourself and your family: a wet butt and a hungry gut!"

I did not wish to argue the point. I had too much respect for Father to doubt the sincerity of his admonition. I knew he meant it for my own good.

As I drove home, I found it impossible to overcome the feeling of uneasiness that Father's words had created deep inside me. What bothered me most was the fact that he had always been right, and, in his mind, I had always been wrong whenever my decisions were contrary to his opinion. It worried me a lot more than I cared to admit, even to myself.

Helping Evelyn with the last-minute packing took my mind off Father's dire predictions, so I pitched in willingly. The children were too small to be of much help; in fact, they were underfoot and in the way most of the time. Evelyn's and my infectious enthusiasm for adventure seemed to rub off on them, and bedlam reigned during those last frantic days before departure.

May 1 arrived at last. Our old Plymouth sedan was packed to its rooftop with all our household belongings, and by the time four children, we parents, and the family cat were aboard, there was not an inch of space left. As a matter of fact, as I drove out of the driveway, the overloaded springs of the car hit rock bottom with a thud that threatened to jar our teeth loose. I guess, to the neighbors, we looked like gypsies, but we felt like adventurers, facing the unknown in search of the pot of gold at the end of the rainbow.

I think I started breathing easier when we drove from the

Holland tunnel onto the Jersey turnpike. Now, at last, we were well on our way, and the vision of Father's anger and his last words to me gradually faded from my mind. In the years that followed, though, I thought of those words many times—and thought, too, how right the old man had been.

It took us three days to drive the almost nine hundred miles to Beaufort. Not that we had any trouble, mechanically or otherwise. We just weren't in any hurry, and each mile we traveled through the states south of New York was new and exciting to us.

Beaufort is a very old, very beautiful town on the South Carolina coast, about midway between Charleston, South Carolina, and Brunswick, Georgia. We had no difficulty finding a place to live, especially since we did not insist on being right in the heart of town. We rented a rambling old farmhouse about three miles north of town. There was a large, shallow lake just to the side of the house. Our nearest neighbor was a farmer about a half mile down a winding dirt road. The farm on which we lived had not been planted for many years, but I learned that it had grown both cotton and tobacco in years gone by. There were beautiful water oaks scattered profusely around the house; our surroundings had a wild, unblemished, natural look, which pleased us greatly. It was so quiet, so different from the noisy bustle of the cities we were used to in New York. Evelyn and I enjoyed especially the quiet, moon-drenched evenings when the lake and the surrounding woods came alive with the bark of foxes, the piercing cry of whippoorwills, the splash of fish, the statuesque blue herons, which stood motionless in the quiet shallows, waiting patiently for a minnow to swim close enough to be gobbled up by a lightning-fast thrust of their long bills.

In Beaufort, I'd found the rustic, almost primitive, land I'd been looking for. I thought that here I had found peace at last. Now all I had to do was make a living.

The day following our arrival in Beaufort I went in search of Captain Harvey and the shrimp fleet. I drove to the south end of town, then across a drawbridge to the island of St. Helena, the home of the shrimpers. I had bought a new set of "work" clothes before leaving New York, so I was wearing what I thought was appropriate garb. It was the same type of clothes I'd worn on the *Dorothy K*: brand new chino shirt, chino pants, creased to a razor's edge, a shiny, wide, rich-brown leather belt, and brand new white canvas deck shoes. On my head was a long-visored chino cap.

A faded, weather-beaten sign, stuck into the ground at the entrance to a dirt road that wound off to my left, indicated that, if I turned there, I would be approaching the home of Captain Jack Harvey.

At the end of the dirt road, I saw two house trailers, then a long bulkhead facing the open bay. There were three trawlers tied in a row alongside the bulkhead. I could make out the names lettered on their sterns: the *Valiant*, the *Victor*, and the *Vagrant*.

Captain Harvey had seen me drive in, and he met me in the yard in front of his trailer. He was a big, ruddy-faced man with a ready smile and bright, sun-crinkled blue eyes. He shook my hand vigorously, then stood studying me from head to toe. I saw his smile broaden, his eyes crinkle even more with unspoken amusement. It think it was my outfit that made him want to burst out laughing. His garb consisted of dirty, grease-smudged, sagging, grey trousers and a once-white tee shirt with a hole in it the size of a golf ball directly over his belly button. He was barefooted and bareheaded. I noticed particularly that my shiny new belt seemed to hold his attention. *His* pants were held up by a length of quarter-inch manila rope. If he had pegged me for a pantywaist dude fresh from the city, I really wouldn't have blamed him, but he made no mention of what it was that amused him. Instead, he said, "Come on, kid, I'll show you around and introduce you to the other men."

We stepped aboard the *Victor*, a fifty-eight-footer. I'd never been on a shrimp boat before, and I was amazed to see the tremendous amount of gear that cluttered her afterdeck: winches, steel cables, buckets, hoses, planks, two or three sets of net "doors," and, from high up in the rigging, a pair of what I assumed to be shrimp nets hanging down to within a foot of the deck. I carefully picked my way through the debris to the pilothouse door. Captain Ilia met us there, and Captain Harvey introduced us. Ilia was a tall, slender, well-built Russian, with heavy black hair and black, piercing eyes. When he spoke, it was with a decided Baltic accent. He, too, was cordial, especially when I told him I'd come from Freeport. Ilia had once owned and operated a beam trawler in the Atlantic off the Long Island coast, having his home port in Baldwin, about three miles west of Freeport.

Captain Harvey and I left the *Victor*, then went aboard the *Valiant* to meet Captain Jimmy. The *Valiant* was about the same size as the *Victor*, but she was a newer boat. Her deck, too, was littered with gear of every description, but there was far more tidiness to the arrangement, indicating to me that her skipper took more pains, and perhaps pride, in keeping her shipshape.

Captain Jimmy was young, about twenty-three or so, and a handsome, bright-eyed lad with a shock of blond, wavy hair that the soiled captain's cap, tilted jauntily at a rakish angle over his left eye, failed to conceal. Jimmy was pleasant, cordial, and seemed genuinely glad to welcome me aboard.

As we approached the last of the three boats, Captain Harvey remarked, "I think I'll let you strike on the *Vagrant* for Charlie. He's been with me a couple of seasons, but this is the first year I'm givin' him his own boat. He can use you to handle the deck work. You can learn a lot from old Poop Deck if you pay him mind."

Poop Deck Charlie, or perhaps now I should call him Captain Poop Deck, was a wiry old codger, around sixty, I guessed, who had all the characteristics of a bantam rooster. When we were introduced, he clasped my hand, danced a little jig on the deck in front of me, and literally welcomed his new striker aboard with open arms. I told him politely that his wife had sent her best regards, to which he answered, "Yeh, boy! Guess old Cactus misses her Poop Deck—misses gettin' tossed in the hay three-four times a week, if the truth was known. Yeh, boy!"

And Charlie again went into his little dance across the deck. I couldn't help laughing at the little rooster. At his age, he just had to be bragging. I was sure old Charlie and I would get along fine.

The *Vagrant* was about the most disreputable looking hulk I have ever seen. She was a former tugboat, a fugitive from the New York Harbor fleet, I imagine, or else she had been put out to pasture because she was too old and too decrepit to do the job she was built for. Her stern deck had nowhere near the depth of the other shrimpers. Her foothigh rail gave me the impression that anything not tied down would wash overboard in the first heavy weather. Her deck was clear of the debris I'd seen on the other boats—I guess it had to be.

Captain Charlie took me below to the narrow, low-ceilinged engine room. Practically every bit of space was taken up by the big thirteen-thousand caterpillar diesel and the heavy-duty, one-cylinder starting motor. Everything in the engine room looked and smelled oily. Even the floorboards squished oil as I stepped gingerly around that big iron beast that was her power.

Charlie kept up a running stream of conversation as he showed me around the *Vagrant*. He was proud of his first command; I could tell that from the way he spoke.

When we returned on deck, my attention was drawn to the *Valiant*, directly astern of the *Vagrant*. Captain Jimmy was on deck talking to a long-legged, busty, bleached blonde, who couldn't have been much more than twenty-two years old. She was draped casually on the forward rail, her drawn-up legs straining the seams of her short-shorts to the breaking point. She wore a flimsy blouse, and, from where I stood, it was evident that the blouse and shorts were all she had on. I guess she figured she didn't need any support underneath. I took a good look and figured she didn't, either.

"Who's that, Charlie?" I asked, nudging my companion.

"Oh, that—that's Elsie—Cap'n Harvey's wife. She visits Jimmy a lot, if you know what I mean."

I wanted to ask more questions, but it was none of my

business. The soft breeze blowing across the *Valiant* brought with it the scent of Elsie's perfume. To me, it wasn't the smell of perfume—it was the smell of trouble.

Poop Deck continued to show me around the boats for the rest of the day, explaining the workings of the cable winches, nets, and various pieces of gear that I would use aboard the *Vagrant*. I headed home around four that afternoon after getting instructions from Captain Harvey to be on deck at five the next morning, ready to go to work.

The following morning, as I drove into the yard, the headlights of my car showed a bustle of activity already under way on the aft decks of the three trawlers. All three boats were sailing that day; it was to be an exploratory excursion to try to locate the beds of shrimp that were expected to move up from the south with the advent of warm weather.

Captain Harvey joined Poop Deck and me aboard the *Vagrant*. Ilia and Jimmy were sailing alone, without benefit of strikers to give them a hand with the deck work.

As we made our way slowly along the dark, winding channels leading to the inlet, Captain Harvey explained the conservation laws that governed shrimping operations.

"We ain't allowed to drag within a mile of the beach," he explained. "The Conservation Department has spotter planes flyin' around all the time, checkin' up on us. If a boat is seen with its nets down inside the mile limit, the plane radios ahead, and a reception committee meets the boat at the dock. There's no use denyin' you were fishin' illegal; those planes got cameras that take pictures of you in the act. It takes a a hell of a lot of shrimp to pay the fines they slap on you. It ain't worth it, especially with the shrimp scarce as they are this time of year. I'd sure like to drag my net in those inshore sloughs we just came through. That's where the shrimp are— up there in the warm water."

The *Vagrant* was the lead boat as we made our way through the gently rolling inlet out into the open sea. The *Victor* was about a hundred yards astern of us, with Captain Jimmy's *Valiant* another hundred yards behind the *Victor*. We had gotten about a half mile offshore when we noticed the *Valiant* had come completely about and was headed back toward the inlet.

"Now where in the hell does he think he's goin'?" Captain Harvey exclaimed. He crossed the stern deck to the pilot-house, where he grabbed up the ship-to-shore radio microphone.

"*Vagrant* to *Valiant*. *Vagrant* to *Valiant*. Come in, Jimmy."

"*Valiant* to *Vagrant*. What's up, Jack?"

"That's what I want to know," Captain Harvey snapped. "You in trouble?"

"Nothin' like that, Skipper. I just remembered—my alarm clock didn't go off this mornin'. I'm goin' into town to get it fixed. I just can't wake up mornin's without a good alarm clock."

Captain Harvey switched off the radio without replying. Instead, he turned to Poop Deck at the wheel.

"Hold her due east, Poop. We can get along without that young pup. If he's too damn lazy to fish, he won't fish. Broken alarm clock, my ass. Who does he think he's foolin'?"

Captain Harvey slammed the pilothouse door on his way

to the stern deck. I looked at Poop Deck, who winked at me slyly.

"That Jimmy'll outsmart himself one of these days," he remarked. "The Skipper's no dope; you can bet on it."

"You mean Jimmy's not goin' into town to get his clock fixed?" I asked naively.

"Hell, no," Charlie replied. "It's Elsie's works he's gonna fix—and not in town, either."

We were just beyond the mile limit when Captain Harvey signaled Charlie to slow down to quarter speed.

"We'll put the try-net over, kid. All you gotta do is watch how it's done."

The try-net was a miniature replica of the big net, which hung from the rigging. It had little wooden "doors" which held the mouth of the eight-foot bag open, its own set of steel cables, and a small-size winch that operated from the drive shaft of the big caterpillar diesel. Captain Harvey explained the necessity for using the try-net.

"We don't put over the big net until we're sure we're over shrimp. We drag the try-net on a steady course for exactly a half hour, then pull her up to see what's on the bottom. If the little net has picked up forty or fifty shrimp, then we put over the big net and go back over the exact same course. The big net is too much trouble to put out and pick up if we ain't sure there's shrimp down there; and besides, there's always the chance we'll get the big net hung up on a sunken wreck or a stob that'll tear up a couple hundred dollars worth of webbin', or we might even snap a cable and lose the whole rig."

We made several half-hour runs with the try-net and picked up blue crabs, spider crabs, small bottom fish, and plenty of black snails—but no shrimp. Around three o'clock in the afternoon, we returned to home port.

During the next few weeks, our fleet of three boats set out each day before daylight to attempt to locate the elusive shrimp, but with very little success. The *Valiant* sailed with us each morning, but more times than not Captain Jimmy found one excuse or another to return to port alone.

Eventually, we managed to pick up a few shrimp in the try-net, but never enough to warrant putting over the big net, which hung lifelessly from the rigging. Captain Harvey gathered together the combined catch from all three boats after one particularly "good" day. We had caught a total of about five pounds of shrimp—hardly enough to take to the packing house. Instead, Captain Harvey packed them carefully in a wax-paper-lined box and took them to the bank in Beaufort. He ceremoniously presented the box to the bank president as a gift. I learned later that the bank held mortgages on the three trawlers and on Captain Harvey's property. This gift-giving was all well and good, but none of us shrimpers had earned a single penny during all these weeks of fishing. As a matter of fact, I had yet to taste my first fresh-caught shrimp.

Late one afternoon we were returning to port after another unsuccessful day when we noticed a group of Negroes frantically waving at us from the grassy bank of the canal that led to our dock. Captain Harvey directed Charlie to pull the *Vagrant* up to the bank to see what had happened.

We learned that a child, a boy of three, had slipped on the slimy mud and fallen into the canal. He had not come to the surface.

"We'll try to find your kid, lady," Captain Harvey assured the mother.

Charlie turned the *Vagrant* about and headed for the mouth of the canal.

"We're gonna put the big net out and drag this here canal," he explained. "We ought to pick up the kid's body— and maybe some shrimp, too. We won't be shrimpin', though, so in case one of those spotter planes flies over, we're fishin' for negras, not shrimps."

I found out then what a difficult job it was to get the large net over the side and into dragging position. I realized that I'd never be able to handle the net alone.

We dragged the entire length of the canal, and, when the huge bag of the net was finally hoisted aboard, the little boy was sitting in the middle of the pocket surrounded by small fish, mud, crabs, and about fifty pounds of shrimp. The boy's eyes were closed; he appeared to be sleeping, but he was dead. The *Vagrant* pulled up to the embankment, and Captain Harvey silently handed the little lifeless form to its mother. The mother acknowledged her gratitude by a simple "Thank you, Suh." The other Negroes stood silently, their heads bowed.

# 5 ~ The Peg-legged Pirate Sails Again

I N SPITE OF ASSURANCES from Captain Harvey and the other skippers that shrimping was bound to improve, I felt I could not wait any longer. After six weeks, I had not earned anything. My finances were such that I knew I had to start earning a living soon.

I believe it was in a waterfront tavern in Beaufort that I heard about a new shrimp boat being built in a St. Augustine shipyard. My source of information was a young fisherman who had just returned from a winter of shrimping in the Gulf of Mexico, in the waters around Dry Tortugas. He assured me that the captain of the new trawler would be looking for a crew. The shrimper was so large, he said, that she'd probably take on at least two strikers.

As I expected, Evelyn was ready, even anxious to move on. Once again, we packed all our belongings and our four kids into the old Plymouth and headed south. New sights, new sounds, new smells; we took them all in and relished every one of them.

I found an inexpensive hotel in St. Augustine for Evelyn and the kids, then proceeded to the waterfront and the shipyard. The new shrimp boat was easily distinguishable among all the other boats in the yard. She was absolutely beautiful—sixty-five feet in length, a twenty-foot beam, glistening white sides, and a varnished deckhouse. Her mast and booms, varnished to a brilliant sheen, seemed to reach halfway to heaven. She had been launched the day before and now lay alongside the bulkhead, her bow pointed eastward toward the open sea. I could see the gold letters across her stern. They read: "*Maria*—Brunswick, Ga."

As I stared up at this beautiful, almost living thing, I saw a small, middle-aged man step from the deckhouse to the port rail. He was dressed in a somber black business suit, white shirt, and dark tie. He clutched a black fedora in his hand.

"Howdy," I called. "Can you tell me where I can find the captain of the *Maria*?"

"I am captain," he answered in a heavy accent. I learned later that he was Portuguese.

"Mind if I come aboard? I'd like to talk to you."

The man did not answer. I took the slight shrug of his shoulders to mean that he couldn't care less, but that if I insisted, it was O.K. with him. I climbed the gangway to the port rail and swung over the rail to the deck. I introduced myself and extended my hand. He ignored it, keeping one hand in his suit pocket, the other still clutching the fedora. After a moment he spoke.

"I am Captain Silva—John Silva. What do you want with me?"

"I'd like to sail with you as striker. Do you need a crew?"

"Got one black man now; need another man. You know how to work shrimp boat?"

I assured him I was an experienced shrimper, having worked with the fleet in South Carolina. Fortunately for me, Captain Silva did not press the interrogation. He seemed to study me closely through half-closed eyes, then said, indifferently, "O.K., you want to work for me, O.K. You be here tomorrow morning. We sail for Brunswick sometime tomorrow."

I was more than a little apprehensive about the whole deal, especially about that dark-eyed, evil-looking cold fish who called himself John Silva. However, I convinced myself that I could put up with an unsocial, unfriendly skipper, so long as I had a chance to sail on that brand new boat.

Now my problem was how to get my family and car to Brunswick. Evelyn did not drive, at least up to that time she didn't. Maybe, I thought, just maybe I could teach her enough about driving in an hour or so that she could drive the car to Brunswick.

I did just that. I showed Evelyn the various gear shifts, showed her how to put in the clutch and put on the brake, taught her to start and stop the motor, then turned her loose. Oh, yes, I did point out Brunswick on the road map.

The following morning, just at daylight, I again stepped aboard the *Maria*. I put my duffle bag on the deck and looked about for some signs of life. In a moment, Captain Silva stepped from the wheelhouse.

"Morning, Cap'n," I greeted. "Where do you want me to stow my gear?"

"You bunk forward—in the forepeak, below deck." He nodded toward a hatch cover forward of the wheelhouse.

I went forward, removed the hatch cover, and descended the iron ladder into the bowels of the hull. In the dim light I could distinguish a port and starboard bunk, which resembled potato bins more than they resembled bunks. I threw my duffle bag into one of the bins, then returned to the deck to seek out Captain Silva.

"I found my bunk, Skipper. Now tell me where to find the mattress that goes on it."

"No mattress," was the surly reply. "I sleep on hard board; you sleep on hard board, too. What for you need mattress?"

I didn't reply. If he couldn't figure out what bare boards would do to my bony frame, I wasn't about to tell him.

I stepped into the aft deckhouse and looked around. It was the galley, all brand spanking new, with the latest equipment. Everything shone and sparkled in stainless steel and enamel. I looked into the cupboards. I found a full set of dishes, pots, and pans of every description—but not a scrap of food. I felt again that wave of apprehension.

Someone stepped into the galley behind me. I turned and faced a Negro youth in his early twenties, tall, broad-shouldered, and built like an athlete. He stood proudly, with his head held high, and looked directly into my eyes. He lacked the stoop-shouldered, apprehensive, even furtive appearance of the average Southern black man. Nor did he have the slow, shuffling gait I'd become used to seeing. This young man walked with a self-assured spring in his step.

I introduced myself and extended my hand. The youth hesitated a fraction of a second, then shook my hand warmly.

"I'm pleased to meet you, Mista Curt," he said sincerely. "My name's Willie. You gonna work on this here boat?"

I assured him that I was.

"That'll be real nice, Mista Curt. I'll be glad to be workin' with you." He gave me a warm smile.

We talked for a while, each volunteering anecdotes of his fishing experiences and trips to sea. I learned that Willie had been working on shrimp boats since he was twelve. I felt that if I were able to gain his friendship I could depend on him to teach me how to handle the gear and to help me over the rough spots.

I looked at my watch. It was almost noon.

"Say, Willie, how about something to eat?"

"I'm with you, Mista Curt. Let's see what we can find." He gave me a wide, toothy grin as he rubbed his stomach.

A search of the immaculate cupboards failed to produce any canned goods or food. The new refrigerator was as bare as the cupboards. Willie and I looked at each other questioningly.

"I'll go ask the captain," I volunteered.

I found Captain Silva in the wheelhouse.

"Say, Cap'n, Willie and I were gonna fix lunch but we can't find the food. You stow it away someplace below deck?"

"No food aboard," Captain Silva replied gruffly. "We catch swimps, we eat. No catch swimps, we don' eat. We sail now."

I gave him the most disgusted look I could muster and returned to the galley and Willie.

"I don't think I'm gonna sail with that cheap mother—" Willie growled. "Let's you and me find us another boat."

"Too late now, Willie," I replied, "Skipper says he's ready to cast off."

The staccato pop-pop-popping sound of the starting motor reached us, giving confirmation to my words. After a few minutes of warming-up time, we heard the slow, heavy thumpty-thump-thump of the big twin caterpillars as Captain Silva meshed the starter's gears into the big diesels. Captain Silva's slight frame appeared in the doorway.

"Wassa matter—you sleep? Get on deck. Cast off, hear?"

Willie and I jumped to obey. Whether we wanted to be or not, we were the *Maria*'s crew.

The big boat glided smoothly from the dock and down the channel at slow throttle. We were not heading for the open sea; Captain Silva apparently had chosen the inland route north to Brunswick.

We had sailed for about three hours through the winding channels and patches of open bay which made up the inland waterway. The countryside was devoid of towns, or even houses, once we'd left St. Augustine. The terrain was flat and marshy; sprawling bushes, palmettos, and salt grass grew along the mud banks, and giant water oaks extended their branches out over the placid water.

Captain Silva, Willie, and I were in the pilothouse. Willie and I conversed in low tones since our polite attempts to include the captain in our conversation were answered with vague grunts or stoic silence.

"How long will it take to get to Brunswick, Willie?" I asked.

"We'll get there tomorrow—tomorrow afternoon, I think."

I rubbed my stomach. "I'll be starved to death by that time," I said ruefully.

I noticed Willie's nostrils flare. He sniffed several times.

"Mista Curt," he said in a low voice, "do you smell somethin'?"

I sniffed too. A slightly acrid odor reached me, but my senses could not identify it immediately. It was a smell of heat, like an empty pot left over an open flame, or the smell of molten lead when I had poured my own fishing sinkers at home.

"Something's mighty hot, Willie," I said, as I continued sniffing the air.

Willie looked at the instrument panel in front of Captain Silva, then grabbed my arm.

"Look there—them water gauges!"

I looked. The needles on the gauges were over to the right as far as they could go. The motor temperatures were well over two hundred and twenty degrees!

Captain Silva seemed to be oblivious to what was going on. I slapped his arm.

"Look, Cap'n—the motors are red hot!" I cried.

He looked at the gauges, then stepped backwards in surprise.

"I think motors run too cold—they burn up too much fuel, so I shut off water intakes. I go turn them on again."

He started for the wheelhouse door, but Willie stuck out his foot, tripping him. The captain went sprawling on the deck just outside the door. Willie threw himself on the prone figure.

"You want to blow us to hell?" he shouted angrily. "You turn on that cold water and that motor'll blow up sky high. Ain't you got no sense in yo' head?"

Captain Silva did not move. Instead, he turned his head to look up at Willie.

"What do we do then?" he asked, fear edging his voice.

"We shuts off them motors and we waits," Willie replied.

Without further conversation, Willie stepped away from the captain and into the wheelhouse. He guided the big boat to the port-side bank of the canal and shut off the motors. Even with the ignition turned off, it took a few minutes for the white-hot motors to cease firing.

I walked to the forward deck and looked around. A hundred yards ahead was a narrow dock jutting out into the channel. A mullet boat, with its nylon net piled high in the stern, was tied to the little dock. On the bank, partially hidden by a growth of pines, was a small cabin.

Willie secured the *Maria* fore and aft to the water oaks that grew along the bank. When he returned on deck, I pointed out the little cabin.

"They're mullet scrappers," he told me, "two brothers by the name of Jackson."

"Do you know them, Willie?"

"I've seen them around the fish house in 'Augustine. They're all right, I guess."

"Come on then," I urged. "Let's go see if they're home. Maybe we can get something to eat."

Willie and I walked to the fishermen's shack without telling Captain Silva of our intention. Neither of us was anxious to have conversation with, or even show consideration to, the surly captain, whose stupidity could easily have caused a horrible tragedy.

I knocked on the cabin door.

"It's open!" a man's voice called from inside.

I pushed open the door and stepped inside. Willie stood outside, a few yards back from the open door.

Virgil and Pete Jackson, both in their late twenties, sat at a kitchen table in the middle of the living room playing cards. An earthen jug stood on the table between them.

"We just came off the shrimper tied up below your dock," I said. "We've got motor trouble and will probably be here awhile."

"What kind of trouble?" the one named Virgil asked.

I explained about the overheated motor.

"That captain of yours sure must be a dumb son of a bitch, and that's a fact," Pete exclaimed. "What say, Virgil, ever hear of anyone dumb enough to turn off water intakes and forget to turn 'em on again?"

"Can't say as I have," Virgil replied. "He's Portugee, ain't he? Never saw a Portugee worth a God-damn; mostly they're meaner'n cat shit, along with bein' dumb."

I had to agree that their opinion of Captain Silva matched my own.

Virgil noticed my friend Willie standing outside the door.

"Who's the nigger?" he inquired.

"That's Willie. He's the other striker on the *Maria*. He's from 'Augustine—says he knows you fellas from around the fish house.

"Hey, Willie—come on in here!" Virgil called.

Willie stepped into the cool, shadowy interior of the cabin.

"Howdy Mista Virgil, Howdy Mista Pete. Nice to see you." Willie's voice was friendly but not deferential. Nei-

ther Virgil nor Pete acknowledged Willie's greeting verbal-
ly, but they nodded slightly. Then Pete asked, "You and
Willie want somethin' to eat?"

"We'd sure be obliged, Pete." I told them about the bare
cupboards and refrigerator aboard the *Maria*.

"Cheap-assed Portugee son of a bitch!" Pete spat out the
words.

We stayed with the Jackson boys all afternoon, and, along
about six o'clock, Willie took over the task of preparing
supper. I don't remember a time when hot biscuits, fried
mullet, and swamp cabbage tasted better. We washed down
the meal with strong, black coffee laced with generous
splashes of corn liquor from the earthen jug. We'd been
sipping from the jug all afternoon, so, by the time supper
was over, I, for one, was feeling no pain. There was a warmth
in my stomach which put a rosy glow on the whole world.
I even felt kindly towards poor Captain Silva, which proves
I must have been a few sheets to the wind.

When it was time to leave the Jackson boys to return to
the *Maria*, I took my wallet from my pocket and removed
a few bills, which I offered to Virgil.

"What's that for?" he inquired.

"Why, hell, I want to pay for that good food and liquor
we had."

Virgil looked at me in disgust.

"You ain't been a fisherman long—not in these parts, anyway. We don't take no pay for feedin' another hungry fisherman. You ain't got no call to offer it, neither. Someday
maybe me and Pete'll be hungry, and we'll come to your
cabin, or on your boat, lookin' for a meal. Then you'll feed

us. We won't offer you no money to pay for it, either. Fishermen take care of each other. That's the way it is; that's the way it's always been."

His words embarrassed me, but taught me a lesson about the kind of men I was to associate with for years to come. I murmured an apology and stuffed the money in my pocket.

Willie and I returned to the *Maria*. I went directly to my bunk below deck to avoid meeting the captain. I was walking a little unsteadily, and I certainly did not want Silva to know I'd had a few drinks and a hearty meal. If he wanted to live up to his own rule of "no catch swimps, we don't eat," that was his business. I was looking out for number one boy —me.

I threw myself into my potato-bin bunk fully clothed. I used my jacket for a pillow, and, while grumbling to myself about how hard and uncomfortable my bed was, I fell sound asleep.

It must have been about 2 A.M. when I was jolted awake by water pouring down on me through the deck above. Before I could scramble to my feet, I was soaked from head to toe. The cabin was pitch dark. I groped my way to the ladder leading to the deck and had climbed up a few rungs when a resounding whack on the top of my head brought stars and the sudden realization that someone had slammed shut the hatch cover. I finally made it to the deck and groped my way aft. It was an inky-black night, but it was not raining. Where did all that water come from? Suddenly there was no longer a deck under my bare feet. I felt myself falling into a hole, and there was nothing in my flailing grasp but empty air. I landed with a thud at the bottom of the hold.

Looking up dazed, with the breath knocked out of me, I saw the dim outline of a face peering down. It was Captain Silva's.

"What you do down there?" he called.

"I fell, you damned fool."

The captain extended his hand, and I pulled myself from the six-foot-deep hold to the deck. I could not stand on my right leg; I thought it was broken. This was not the case, however. I had hit my leg on the edge of one of the shrimp bins as I fell and had severely bruised the bone, in addition to scraping off a strip of hide about six inches long.

"I took off hatch cover to wet down bilge," Captain Silva explained. "Why you on deck, anyway?"

"I got wet. Water suddenly came pouring down on me through the deck seams."

Captain Silva laughed for the first and only time during our brief acquaintance.

"Oh, that! I hose down deck so seams swell up. New boat, seams not tight yet."

"Why hose it in the middle of the night right over my bunk?" I asked, anger in my voice.

"Better at night," he explained, unruffled. "Sun no dry up seams at night." Again he laughed, unperturbed by my discomfort.

I limped to the forward hold, my leg throbbing. I was wet, angry, and thoroughly disgusted.

It took almost forty-eight hours for the temperature inside the caterpillar diesels to cool sufficiently for us to continue our journey north. It was a long, tiresome wait, and my anxiety grew with each passing hour. I wondered if

Evelyn and the kids had made it safely to Brunswick. Had they found a place to stay? Were they worried because we were almost two days overdue?

We continued our journey along the inland waterway until, at long last, the city of Brunswick could be seen on the horizon. The end of our journey was in sight! Willie's and my spirits rose considerably.

Suddenly, in mid-channel, the *Maria* started turning in a huge circle. Willie and I looked at each other. He shook his curly head as if to say, "I don't know; you tell me!" and headed to the wheelhouse. I followed closely behind.

"What's wrong now, Cap'n?" I asked Silva, who stood at the wheel studying a chart spread out in front of him.

"That marker over there," he said, pointing to starboard. "It don't belong there. These channel markers are all wrong."

"How do you know?" I asked, belligerently.

"I sail these waters twenty years ago. I remember good. Those markers not in same place."

Why, you stupid ass, I said to myself, channels change in twenty years. Markers are moved to meet those changes. How dumb can one man be? Aloud I said, "What are you going to do?"

"I go in circles. Soon another boat come along, maybe. Then I follow him into Brunswick."

Willie and I looked at each other and grinned. The situation was so disgusting it was funny. We were so near home, and yet so far.

We finally made it into port. As we secured the mooring lines, I saw Evelyn and the kids standing beside the old Plymouth. Gee, it was good to see them!

Willie and I gathered our gear and stepped out on deck. Captain Silva stood at the rail.

"Where you go?" he inquired of both of us.

"I quit," I said. "Willie does too. We've had about all of you we can take."

"Oh?" snarled Silva. "You don' want to work. You both lazy bums. You jus' want free ride to Brunswick!"

Willie grabbed my arm and held on. He knew I would have slugged that nasty little Portugee, even if I had to go to jail for it!

# 6 ~ The Green Seas

EVELYN HAD RENTED a furnished bungalow on Saint Simon's Island, about ten miles from the shrimp docks at Brunswick. The route to the island was over a causeway which crossed through marshland, through fields of feather grass and cattails, and over rustic little bridges to a sleepy resort village.

Evelyn was fascinated by my adventures aboard the *Maria*. I, in turn, was amazed by her ability to drive all the way from St. Augustine to Brunswick without a driver's license and without incident. It took nerve, and I gave her credit for making it.

"Well," she exclaimed, after we'd told each other our respective stories, "what do we do now? Have you gotten your belly full of shrimpers?"

"No," I answered resolutely, "I haven't had a chance to learn what shrimping is all about. Not yet, anyway. I still think there's money to be made. I'll try again."

Evelyn shook her head, but said nothing. I guess she figured if she gave me enough rope . . .

The following morning I drove to the Brunswick shrimp docks. There were about twenty boats tied up at the various packing houses; fishermen were mending nets, stowing gear, loading ice in the ships' deep holds; all sorts of preparations were being made for setting out for the shrimp grounds. A small group of men were sitting on fish boxes playing cards just inside the open doors of one of the packing houses. I walked up to them.

"Howdy," I said, pleasantly, "I'm looking for work. Any of you fellas know of a boat needing a striker?"

Two of the card players put their cards face down on the table and looked me over carefully.

"You a shrimper?" one of them inquired.

"I worked some in Carolina. Came in on the *Maria* yesterday. I was going to work for John Silva but changed my mind."

The men looked at each other and grinned.

"You got sense, boy—good sense. I wouldn't fish with that Portugee for all the shrimp in the ocean."

The others murmured agreement.

"Seems I heard Woody is lookin' for a striker," the other man said. "That's Captain Woodrow Nelson—owns the *Green Seas*. She's tied up down at the end of the dock."

I thanked them for the information and hurried to the end of the long pier. I found the *Green Seas*, a thirty-foot, narrow-beamed hulk that had been a pleasure boat at one time, but, with the addition of a mast, boom, and donkey engine on the stern deck, was now a working shrimp boat. Her stern hatch was open, and I could see a shock of blond, curly hair bobbing about in the hold. I stepped aboard and called, "Hi, Skipper!"

A boyish face looked up and scowled.

"I'm looking for work," I said. "Understand you need a striker."

The face no longer scowled, neither did the man smile.

"You a shrimper?" he asked, without enthusiasm.

I told him of my limited experience, but was careful not to say just how limited.

"I can use a striker—if ever I get this shaft lined up. Got a bad whip in it; she gets to shakin' real bad at full throttle."

"Anything I can do to help?" I asked.

"Stick around if you want. We'll try her out in a minute, soon as I tighten up these bolts."

When Captain Nelson finally lifted himself up out of the hold, I saw a stockily built, heavyset man in his early thirties. His broad, open face could have been friendly and pleasant, but for reasons known only to himself, the captain chose to scowl, tight-lipped, rather than smile. He stood looking me over, but said nothing. He turned abruptly and strode toward the wheelhouse.

"Get ready to cast off," he called over his shoulder.

Within a few minutes we were under way, moving slowly down the canal to the bay. When we reached open water, Woody opened the throttle, bidding me watch the propeller shaft to see if any whipping occurred. It did. The entire hull shook. Woody reduced speed.

"Shaft's out of line. Nothin' I can do about it, just let it whip."

I said nothing. The thought crossed my mind that Woody couldn't be much of a fisherman, neglecting a serious defect in his boat that way. There was another thing that strengthened that opinion of my new skipper. The *Green Seas* was powered by an eight-cylinder Chrysler Royal gasoline motor. She carried a small tank of gas all right, but she also had two built-in tanks for diesel fuel. Captain Woody would start the Chrysler on gasoline, then shut off the water intakes long enough to get the motor red hot. Then he would turn on the diesel fuel and maintain an extremely high temperature within the motor so that the spark plugs would fire the diesel fuel, thus avoiding the high cost of gasoline. Incredible as it may seem, he got away with it—for a while, anyway.

The day following our shakedown cruise we took to the open sea to try our luck at shrimping. Captain Woodie did not bother with a try-net; we put over the large net as soon as we were a mile offshore. We dragged all day, picking up the net at about two-hour intervals.

My first experience in picking up that big, cumbersome, heavy net was nearly a tragedy for me. We had retrieved the length of cable and the doors by means of the power winch and had the net alongside. The next operation consisted of getting a rope "strap" around the webbing, hooking a cable to it, and hoisting it on board by means of block and tackle. Woodie instructed me to encircle the net with the strap while he handled the block and tackle. We were broadside to the rolling ground swell, and when the boat rolled toward the net, I grabbed the webbing and tried to haul it over the rail. The boat rolled away from the net, and instead of letting go, I held on. The net slid over the side, and so did I. I went under, arms and legs thrashing, becoming more and more entangled in the net. Woodie pulled me out eventually, and, instead of asking if I was hurt, he said, scowling as usual, "You're pretty stupid, ain't you?"

From then on, I was careful to brake the net tightly across the rail whenever the boat rolled away from the net.

Our catch that day consisted of thousands of pounds of jellyfish, bottom fish of every description, about two hundred pounds of blue-claw crabs, and thirty pounds of shrimp.

I learned that day what a dirty, messy job shrimping was. When the bag was emptied on deck, it was my job to pick through the muck, slime, and jellyfish to retrieve what few shrimp were there, then shovel the rest of the debris overboard. No matter how much filthy garbage the net spewed out on the deck, Woody never once gave me a hand. If it took me two hours to sort shrimp and clean each time we picked up the net, Woody remained in the pilothouse reading a book or magazine. Another thing that was particularly annoying to me was that somehow Woody always managed to have lunch prepared just when it was time to pick up the net. My lunch, usually consisting of fried eggs and grits, would lie in the cold frying pan for at least two hours before I got a chance to eat it. Cold fried eggs drenched in re-used grease and cold, congealed grits did not set well in my stomach, especially on a rolling sea.

After the shrimp were separated from the mud and slime, it was my job to "head" them before packing them in ice. Heading consisted of snipping off the shrimp's head between thumb and forefinger with the thumbnail. This was not a hard job, but it had to be done barehanded. Shrimp have tiny spines and a sharp shell covering around their heads, and as a result of heading them, my fingers suffered hundreds of tiny cuts, none deep enough to draw blood, just deep enough to become infected from the jellyfish and muck I dug through all day long. Eventually, I developed fish poisoning, as it was called among the fishermen. My hands and arms became so badly infected that I was laid up for two weeks, both hands so swollen I could neither feed nor dress myself.

During those first three weeks as striker on the *Green*

*Seas*, I earned about eight dollars a day for twelve hours' work. Five of the eight dollars came from selling the blue crabs I had accumulated in a fifty-five-gallon drum we had lashed to the starboard rail. Actually, I got ten dollars for the two hundred pounds of crabs I trundled down to the crab processing house each evening, but Captain Woodrow reminded me that he was entitled to half. The other three dollars a day I received was my share of the day's catch of shrimp.

Woody continued to be unfriendly, sour of disposition, and uncommunicative. He arrived at the boat on his bicycle at five each morning, left on his bike upon our return to the dock each evening, and I doubt that we exchanged a score of words all day. He spent almost the entire day in the wheel-house with his magazines and paperback novels, while I was on the stern deck amid jellyfish, mud, slime, stingrays, and —oh yes—a few handfuls of shrimp. By this time, I was pretty well fed up with shrimping in general—and Captain Woodrow and his *Green Seas* in particular.

I believe it was on a Thursday morning that the straw came that finally broke the camel's back. I'd arrived at the dock at four forty-five that morning, and, promptly at five, Captain Woody came around the corner of the fish house on his bicycle. The wire basket on the handlebars was loaded with bags of groceries.

"Boy, oh, boy, Cap'n," I exclaimed, "looks like we're going to eat good today!"

"What d'ya mean, today?" he snapped in his usual surly tone. "We'll be gone until Sunday."

Panic seized me. "Sunday!" I yelled in surprise. "You

didn't tell me we wouldn't be home tonight, same as usual."

"That's just too bad," he snarled. "Maybe I forgot to tell you. Come on, get those groceries aboard." He disappeared into the wheelhouse without another word.

We left the dock accompanied by a half dozen other shrimp boats from the fleet. As we passed within a hundred yards of the St. Simon's Island city dock, I had half a mind to jump overboard and swim ashore. I didn't, though. I guess I was too mad and too stubborn to give Woody the satisfaction.

We put the big net over when we were about two miles offshore. I noticed on the way out that we had taken a northeasterly course, rather than sailing due east as we usually did. I guessed that Woody had decided to drag in a new, untried territory.

There was nothing that required my attention for the next few hours, so I sat on the stern deck with my back resting against the wheelhouse wall. I stared out at the tightly stretched steel cables that held the net dragging invisibly on the bottom. The protesting whine of the straining motor reached my ears from below deck. I knew from the smell of scorching metal and the exhaust fumes that Captain Woody had shut down the water intakes and was running on diesel fuel.

Hah, I thought, he thinks he's saving money by burning diesel oil instead of gas. He'll burn out that Chrysler inside of three months, if I'm any judge. Serve him right, the cheap bastard.

Then I started thinking about the surprise he'd pulled on me that morning.

So we won't be home 'til Sunday, I mused. What a lousy trick that was. Oh, yeah, he forgot to tell me, did he? Bullshit. He just didn't give a damn whether I knew ahead of time or not. Wish now I'd jumped overboard at St. Simon's dock. Evelyn and the kids'll be worried sick.

I continued my self-indulgent musing, and the longer I thought about it, the angrier I got.

Just suppose, I thought, we were to get that net hung up on a stob or a sunken wreck. We'd tear up; then we'd have to go back home. Maybe if I concentrate hard enough, I can whammy the net into hanging up.

I stared at the rolling sea astern, at the spot I judged the invisible net to be.

"Come on, net, come on. Hang up, will you?"

I was dumfounded to see the steel cables suddenly stretch, then slacken, then stretch, then slacken again. I could hardly keep the grin off my face. I arose leisurely from the deck and walked to the wheelhouse door.

"Hey, Cap'n—I think we might be hung up."

Captain Woodrow immediately shut down the throttle, put the motor into neutral, and followed me on deck.

"We'll pick up," he ordered.

When the net, or rather what was left of it, was on deck, we found it was less than half its original length. It was definitely beyond repair.

"Too bad, Skipper," I lied. "Guess we'll have to go back home now, huh?"

"I got a new net in the hold. We'll hang it in. Cut those doors loose."

An hour later, I was again alone on the stern deck watching the cables as we dragged the new net.

"O.K., net, whammy one more time! I did it once, maybe I can do it again. Come on, net, hang up, dammit!"

It did. This time the cables stretched until I thought surely either they or the boom would snap. I watched, fascinated, as they strained to the breaking point, then suddenly went slack. Again, I walked to the wheelhouse with assumed nonchalance to inform Woody that I thought we might have hung up.

Again we raised the net. Again we had nothing but fragments of webbing between the doors at the ends of the cables.

"Well, Cap'n, there goes about three hundred bucks worth of webbing." I tried not to sound as triumphant as I felt. "Guess we've got to go back in to Brunswick."

Captain Woodrow said nothing. He went into the wheelhouse, slamming the door behind him.

We did not head home; not just then, anyway. Instead, Woody steered the *Green Seas* alongside one of the other Brunswick boats which had been dragging parallel to us about a half mile away. The captain of the other shrimper was a close friend of Captain Woodrow. He sympathized with us in our misfortune and told Woody he would be glad to lend us one of his spare nets. Within the hour, we were dragging again.

"Well, net," I said aloud, when I was alone again on the stern deck, "we did it twice. Think we can do it one more time? Come on, net, hang up—just once more. Come on, whammy, do it again for li'l Daddy!"

I stared at the sea, my brows furrowed in concentration. I couldn't do it three times in a row, not in a million years, but I did—you'd better believe I did. This time, when the net became snagged on some hidden obstruction, the weakened cables stretched to their maximum endurance, then snapped. We had nothing left but the broken ends of twisted cable hanging from the boom.

We headed back to Brunswick. I suppose I should have felt compassion for Captain Woodrow, but, at the time, I didn't. I was relieved to step ashore from the *Green Seas* that afternoon, for the last time. I didn't have to tell Woody I'd quit. I'm sure he knew it. I've often wondered if he realized I was the cause (the wish being father to the deed) of his losing thousands of dollars worth of rigging that day, just because he did not show me the consideration I thought I deserved.

I later heard that about a week after I sailed with Woody on the *Green Seas* for the last time, he went to sea alone to drag his new net. He was on deck hoisting the net; the Chrysler motor, running on diesel fuel, was idling in neutral. Suddenly the motor blew up, tearing a gaping hole in the side of the hull. Captain Woodrow was thrown overboard by the force of the explosion but managed to swim away from the debris before the *Green Seas* went down. He was picked up, unharmed, by another shrimper.

On the morning after I left the *Green Seas*, I had a leisurely breakfast at home with Evelyn and the kids and returned to the shrimp docks. I had no intention of trying for a striker's job on any of the other shrimp boats. I had gotten my belly full of bad-tempered captains, fish poisoning, and empty pockets. Again I thought of Father's dire prediction of what a fisherman's life would be. I'd gotten the wet butt all right; the hungry gut was only a few hundred dollars away, not only for me, but for my family.

I sauntered along the dock taking in the sights and smells that had, by now, become familiar to me. As I made my way around piles of net, cable, and various pieces of gear that cluttered the walkway, I called out greetings to several of the captains and strikers I'd come to know. When I neared the end of the dock, I saw my colored friend Willie sitting on a fish box mending net. The wooden shuttle filled with mending twine seemed to fly in his experienced fingers, and his pace did not slacken when he looked up and grinned at me.

"Hi, Mista Curt! What you doin' on the beach? Thought you'd be out fishin' t'day."

I told Willie of my experiences on the *Green Seas*. He listened attentively, and, when I told of my ability to whammy the net three times in succession, his eyes rolled, he whacked his thigh, and his loud burst of laughter caused the men on the nearby boats to look up from their work and grin.

"My, oh my, Mista Curt, if you don't beat all! You got yourself a whammy, sho' 'nough!" And again he burst into laughter.

After Willie had savored my story to the fullest, I asked, "You're not fishing these days, Willie?"

"No, suh, I ain't goin' out. Ain't 'nough shrimp out there this time o' year. I makes more sittin' here on the dock mendin' nets for the other fishermen to tear up. Might be I'll go out when the colored boys brings their boats down from Thunderbolt. They won't be here for another month or so. Tell you the truth, I'd ruther fish on a colored boat." Willie was silent for a moment, concentrating on the swiftly moving shuttle in his hand. Then he looked up at me again.

"What you gonna do now, Mista Curt?"

"I don't know for sure, Willie. All I know is that I'm fed up to here with shrimping. Reckon I'd best be moving on, but I don't know just where to go."

Willie said nothing. The shuttle continued to fly through the meshes of the net he was mending.

"What I'd really like to do, Willie," I said as I wound twine on a spare shuttle I retrieved from Willie's back pocket, "is to try net fishing—gill netting, inside, in some bay or river. Where would you suggest I go?"

Willie thought for a long moment, then scratched his head with the end of his shuttle.

"I reckon you'd find what you're lookin' for down 'round Fort Pierce on the Indian River. They does gill nettin' down there year 'round, and I hear they does pretty good. You wants to go down to Florida?"

"I'm willing to try it. How about you, Willie—want to go gill net fishing with me?"

Willie hesitated only briefly.

"Why shore, Mista Curt. I's willin', iff'n you wants me to go. I'll have a chance to see my folks in Sanford before we're ready to start fishin'."

And so it was arranged. Willie would go on to Sanford, Florida, and I would meet him there within the week. I was not sure just where we'd end up, but I was ready and anxious to head for new horizons.

I hummed and whistled all the way home that afternoon.

# 7 ~ On to Florida

MY FAMILY and I left St. Simon's Island three days later, without regret. Shrimping had been a terrible disappointment, and I was ready to put as much distance between me and the Brunswick docks as I could. The dreams I had had of a financial bonanza as a shrimper never materialized, and I felt I'd wasted enough time. Certainly there were other fish in the sea; all I had to do was learn how to catch them.

We drove leisurely to the small town of Sanford in northern Florida and were able to find Willie's parents' home on the outskirts of town. Willie threw a battered suitcase into the back of our car, and we were off to the East Coast and Fort Pierce. Even with the addition of another passenger, the Plymouth did not seem overcrowded. Somehow, our possessions were slowly, but surely, diminishing. We'd found that a lot of the baggage we'd taken from New York could be eliminated. We were now down to a few suitcases.

Fort Pierce was a bustling little seaport town; her waterfront docks were lined with huge freighters and tankers which came from the open sea through the deep, wide, well-protected Fort Pierce Inlet. Willie and I strolled along the docks looking for evidence of the gill-net fishing boats, but we soon learned that the majority of commercial fishermen did not work out of Fort Pierce; they worked out of the smaller villages to the south, along the Indian River.

We drove south on highway 1-A, which followed along the bank of the river. About fifteen miles south of Fort Pierce we came to the community of Jensen Beach, nestled comfortably on the west bank of the river. In the center of the village was Pitchford Brothers' Fish House. Surrounding the fish house were racks filled with drying nets. Anchored just offshore was a fleet of flat-bottomed, outboard-driven net boats.

"This looks like it, Willie," I exclaimed. "Let's ask around."

We stopped at the fish house, and, while Willie remained outside, I went in. A fisherman in rubber overalls and knee-high boots was loading and weighing mullet in hundred-pound boxes.

"Howdy," I said by way of greeting. "Mind if I ask you a couple questions?"

"Sure, go ahead," he answered. "What's on your mind?"

"I'd like to find out about getting a gill-net rig. I'm looking for some used net and a boat. Have any idea if there's an outfit for sale around here?"

"Don't rightly know, not here in Jensen, anyway. The boys is all usin' the outfits they got." He hesitated, thinking. "You might try the fish house in Salerno. They could maybe fix you up."

I thanked him, and after learning that Salerno was about seven miles further south, I returned to the car.

Salerno was a community of a few fishermen's shacks and a fish house set on pilings extending out into the river. Willie and I walked into the fish house and approached two men, dressed like the fishermen at Jensen Beach, who were loading and weighing fish. I told them what I was looking for.

"Yeah," said one, "I got some net I can sell you. It's up there in the loft. If y'all can wait a bit, I'll fetch it down."

When he had finished weighing out a hundred pounds of mullet in the box that rested on the platform scales, he climbed a ladder to the loft.

"Watch your head," he called.

He threw several bundles of net to the floor below, climbed down, and stood beside the nets.

"These is hundred-yard shots," he explained. "They's three-inch mesh, hung in for mullet scrappin'. How much net you think you'll be needin'?"

"What are most of the boys using?"

"Three, four, maybe five hundred yards," he replied. "It depends on where you'll be scrappin'."

"How much you asking for it?"

"Now this here's a fine linen net. I'll let you have it for, say, twenty dollars a shot."

"O.K.," I said, "I'll buy five hundred yards; that is, if Willie, here, thinks it's in good enough condition to fish with."

Willie, who had said nothing during the transaction, squatted down alongside the net. He placed his thumb and forefinger between one of the meshes and strained to break it. It did not break. He picked up several other lengths of webbing and tested them the same way. None of the meshes were weak enough to break.

"It looks O.K.," he said, without enthusiasm.

I turned to the fisherman.

"You got yourself a deal."

I handed him a hundred dollars from my wallet.

"You don't happen to have a boat that you'd sell me, do you?"

"Just happens I do," the fisherman replied. "I got two outfits; can't use but one."

He took me outside to the narrow stretch of sandy beach along the water's edge. We walked to a twenty-foot, flat-bottomed, grey-painted hull that looked for all the world like an oversized rowboat. Its forty-horsepower Johnson outboard was set in a well forward of midships in the boat. From the motor well, aft, it was completely open and un-cluttered. There was no stern deck, just the top edge of the transom.

"I'll take three hundred for her," he volunteered. "Sound as a dollar, she is. Motor's in A-1 shape; just had it over-hauled."

I looked at Willie before committing myself. Together we went over the hull carefully, looking for signs of dry rot or wormy planking. She seemed sound enough, so I decided to buy. This time, though, I thought I'd dicker a bit before handing over my money.

"She looks in fair shape," I admitted; "not worth three hundred, though. I'll give you two."

"Two seventy-five. She's worth all of that."

"Two and a quarter."

"Two fifty. Not a cent less. Besides, you gotta have a boat to carry all that net you just bought," he added, slyly.

I caught a slight nod from Willie out of the corner of my eye.

"O.K.," I said, "it's a deal. Let's go back inside."

In the fish house I handed over the money. The fisherman took two folded green papers from his well-worn wallet.

"This here's the registration and title," he explained. "I'll sign 'em over, iff'n you got a pen."

I did, and the transaction was completed.

During the entire time we had been with the fisherman, he had ignored Willie's presence completely. Now, after a quick glance in Willie's direction, he turned his back to Willie and spoke to me.

"Say, now," he said, unsmiling, "there's just one more thing. You fixin' to take that nigra fishin' with you?"

"Why, sure," I answered, surprised at the bluntness of the question. "Anything wrong with that?"

"We just don't cotton to no nigras on our river," he said. "We don't want 'em out there fishin' with us. Iff'n any of them does, they're liable to end up gettin' hurt."

"Why is that?" I asked, embarrassed for my friend's sake.

"We just don't allow it, is all. That there river is for white fishermen. Another thing—if you want to sell your fish, you'll leave that nigra on the beach. Otherwise, ain't no fish house, includin' us or the Pitchfords, will buy from you."

I was completely flabbergasted. I had counted heavily on Willie's knowledge of nets and fishing to get me started as a gill netter. Now I wasn't sure I could learn enough on my own to make a success of it. I had one more question.

"How come the shrimp boats from Florida to the Carolinas take colored men on their boats? Some even have crews made up entirely of colored."

"That's different," replied the fisherman, patiently. "Them shrimp boats fishes out in the ocean. We figger the ocean's big enough so's anybody, even nigras, can fish out there."

"Why do you hate the colored folks so much?" I couldn't help asking the question.

"Now whatever gives you yankees the idea we hate 'em? We don't hate nigras. We don't exactly love 'em, but so long as they stay in their place, and don't try to mix in with white folks where they're not wanted, we all get along just fine. Maybe someday you yankees'll figger out that blacks is black and whites is white, and they don't mix. We don't have no trouble with our nigras. They're satisfied to stay by theirselves, and we leave 'em alone. You got any more questions?"

I didn't. Willie and I returned to the car.

"Don't you feel bad, Mista Curt," Willie said kindly. "You had no way of knowin' they felt that way about colored folks. I ain't gonna do nothin' to get you in trouble with them fishermen, so I guess I'll go back to Brunswick. I can do like I planned; I can mend nets 'till the boys from Thunderbolt get there. They're good Georgia colored boys; they'll give me lots of work."

I had to admit Willie's decision made good sense. That evening I bought Willie's bus ticket back to Georgia. I was sorry to see him go; he was a good friend.

The following day I returned to Salerno to get my new boat and nets. I returned with it to Jensen Beach, where I moored it in a vacant place behind Pitchfords' Fish House. On several occasions during the next three days, I went out with my boat and nets, but, try as I might, I could not locate fish. I dropped my net in what I thought were likely areas, but the result was a total disappointment. I spoke to several gill netters at the fish house and learned that night was the proper time to gill net. As a matter of fact, the only time. Their heavily laden mullet boats proved the truth of their theory. I decided to try it.

That evening I ran my net out from the river bank in front of the little cottage we had rented. I anchored one end of the net on shore; the other end, I anchored and buoyed about three hundred yards offshore. I went home and went to bed.

The following morning, bright and early, I stood on the river bank hauling in my net. I nearly jumped for joy at what I found. During the night, I had caught about a hundred pounds of fish, including mullet, trout, redfish, and flounder. I loaded the catch into my boat and sailed to the fish house unloading dock.

"Whatcha got, fisherman?" Joe Pitchford called down to me good-naturedly.

"Send down a basket, Joe. Better get a couple strong boys on that block and tackle up there. I got me a pretty good mess."

When the fish were hauled up on the loading platform, Joe started to dump them into one of the enormous chill boxes, but he hesitated and set the basket down on the platform. He picked a trout from the basket, opened its gill covers, then brought it up to his nose. He sniffed, then threw the trout on the platform. He repeated the process with several mullet, then another trout. After each sniff his nose crinkled, and he threw the fish aside in disgust.

"Where'd you say you got these fish?" he asked.

"Why, in the river—last night."

"Tell me what you did."

I told Joe how I'd set my net at sundown, gone home, then returned in the morning to haul in my net.

"No wonder they stink," Joe said, derisively. "They're rotten. Don't you know better'n to leave fish hangin' in a net all night?"

I admitted I didn't.

"The warm water rots 'em. Rots 'em fast. Remember, that river water is about eighty degrees this time of year. Then, too, there was a bright moon last night. Don't you know that moonlight can rot fish as quick as sunlight? Maybe even quicker."

"Gosh, Joe, I didn't know. Hell, here I thought I had it made. Set my net out in the evening, go home to bed with the old lady all night, then haul in a net full of fish the next morning. You must think I'm pretty stupid."

"You'll learn, kid, you'll learn," Joe said, not unkindly. "Ain't no kind of fishin' comes easy. Those other gill netters that sell to us work damn hard for a livin'. They're out there all night long, workin' every minute. They search out a school of fish, run their net around them, pick up the net, then search out another school. It ain't easy, believe me."

"I can see that. Well, I'll try to do better next time. At least I'll work at it. I sure won't try to pass off rotten fish on you again."

"You didn't know, kid. We'll forget about it."

For the next several weeks I spent almost every night out on the river. I learned to glide my boat quietly in the shadows along the mangroves that lined the river bank. I located schools of mullet by their silvery flashes as they leaped and splashed in the moonlight. Sometimes I was lucky enough to get my net around a small school; other times, in fact more often than not, they managed to elude me. The Pitchford Brothers' Fish House bought all the fish I brought in, and I was able to average twenty-five to thirty dollars a week, fishing six nights.

# 8 ~ I Become a Seiner

O NE AFTERNOON I was at the fish house talking to Joe Pitchford when he surprised me by asking, "How'd you like a job?"

"Doing what, Joe?"

"Fishin'. We own a seine rig here in Jensen. Captain Tobey runs it for us. He's shorthanded a man, and if you'd be interested, he might take you on. It takes a three-man crew, and you'd most likely do better, moneywise, than you're doin' now, fishin' by yourself."

"Sounds fine, Joe," I exclaimed. "Where do I find Captain Tobey?"

"Walk down along the river, south, about a half mile. You'll see some net racks, a little shack we use to store gear in, and," Joe looked at his watch, "Tobey and his partner Kenny ought to be mendin' net down there just about now."

I thanked Joe and hurried out the door. It was not difficult to find the seine rig. I saw a narrow dock extending out into the river from a small shack partially hidden in a cluster of mangroves. There were several boats tied up at the little dock; I saw two open launches about twenty-four feet in length, three or four rowboats, and a net boat. The net boat interested me. It was built like an oversized rowboat, about twenty-four feet in length, fully eight feet wide, and flat-bottomed. It was completely devoid of seats, lockers, or afterdeck.

As I approached the landing, I saw two men pulling a grey-black net from the dock railing into the net boat. I introduced myself to the older of the two men.

"Captain Tobey?" I inquired. "Joe Pitchford sent me down to find you; says you might need another man on your seine rig."

"Ya," Tobey replied, extending his hand, "I do need another hand."

His accent seemed to be Scandinavian. I learned later that Tobey was from Finland. He paused; each of us looked the other over. I liked Tobey instantly—liked his big, round, open face, his humor-filled blue eyes, his friendly, warm smile. I judged him to be in his early fifties. His heavy thatch of short-cropped hair was iron-grey. Tobey was heavyset, built like a wrestler. With each movement of his arms, the muscles in his shoulders and barrel chest heaved and rippled. Tobey turned to the other man working beside him.

"This is my partner Kenny," he said.

We shook hands. Kenny was in his late twenties, a short man, only about five-five, with a sun-reddened face which looked for all the world like the face of an ape—a very friendly ape. His body, too, was apelike. When he stood erect, his muscular shoulders hunched forward; his heavy arms hung to his knees. I learned later that from the time Kenny was about seven years of age he had worked with his father on a seine rig in Hobe Sound. Seining was illegal in Palm Beach County, so their operations had to be carried on at night, in complete silence and secrecy. They could not use their boat motors to haul in the net; it had to be done by hand. None of those illegal fishermen ever dared to smoke while they were working. They feared the odor of tobacco smoke would carry on the night air to the sensitive noses of the game wardens. Instead of smoking, the fishermen chewed tobacco.

Kenny did too—constantly. Pulling in the heavy net night after night during his formative years had stretched Kenny's arms to abnormal lengths and had developed his chest, shoulder, and arm muscles to the point of being muscle-bound.

"Have you done any fishing?" Tobey asked me.

I told him something of my background and experience with boats and fishing.

"You can fish with us if you like," Tobey said. "We pay the Pitchfords the boat share of one-third; we take out gas and oil expenses; then we share alike."

"That sounds fine to me," I said. "Maybe now I can give you a hand pulling that net off the rail."

For the next two hours I worked with my new partners, pulling the heavy net into the net boat. The seine, Kenny told me, was fifteen hundred yards long, twelve feet deep, made of heavy linen, and tarred and salt-cured for preservation. Its lower edge was heavily weighted with evenly spaced leads, its top edge buoyed with evenly spaced round corks. In the center of the seine, a heavy, close-meshed bag with a twelve-foot opening extended out behind the net for about twenty feet. As Kenny explained it, when both ends of the net were hauled in simultaneously, the decreasing circumference of the circle drove the fish into the bag. I noticed as I helped pull the net into the boat that there were three-foot lengths of ⅜-inch manila rope spliced into the cork line at about thirty-foot intervals.

"Those are straps," Kenny explained. "When the net is overboard and being dragged along by the two launches, your job will be to work yourself around the net in a sloopie (rowboat) and tie the straps to the rope we use to haul in the net. We don't pull the net in by hand; we use the nigger-head spool on the donkey engines in each of the launches."

To me it looked like an exciting adventure. The prospect of working with a net almost a mile long, with two experienced, seasoned fishermen, seemed to be the answer to my fondest dreams. I was ready to go right then and there and told Captain Tobey so.

"We go out tomorrow morning. The tide will be right about four o'clock. We will meet here at three in the morning. Meantime, let's go up to Pitchfords' for a beer. You drink beer, don't you?"

I said I did, on occasion.

"That's good," Tobey said, smiling. "You fish with us, you drink lots of beer."

I soon found out what he meant. We walked up the dusty road the half mile to Pitchfords' Fish House, the front part of which was a beer joint. We took one of the booths near the door.

"Three Ballantines, Joe," Kenny called, making himself comfortable on the hard wooden bench.

I reached into my back pocket for my wallet. Tobey put a restraining hand on my arm.

"We don't pay no money for beer. We pay with beer fish. Now that you're one of us, you drink all you want, but you never pay."

"What are beer fish?" I asked.

"Every day we go out," Tobey explained, "we take out an extra sloopie. When we bail fish out of the net, we throw a scoopful of fish into the beer sloopie every once in a while, 'til we got seventy-five, maybe a hundred pounds of beer fish. We bring them in to Joe, give them to him for free. Then we drink all the beer we want, for free."

"Who comes out ahead?" I asked.

Tobey shrugged and laughed. "I think we break even, most of the time. Maybe we're ahead, just a little bit." We all laughed.

The following morning, a few minutes before three, I drove to the landing where I was to meet Captain Tobey and Kenny. They were already there; I could see their silhouettes out on the end of the dock.

Kenny left the landing in his launch soon after I arrived, towing the net boat and three sloopies behind him. He pulled away from the dock about a hundred feet and lay to, with his motor idling, until Tobey and I cast off. We glided past Kenny's launch, and, as we did so, Kenny threw me his bow line.

"Make it fast to the stern post," he called.

I caught the rope and hastened to throw a couple of clove hitches around the wooden post in the stern deck. Thus secured, we pulled away from the landing, Tobey's launch towing the others in tandem. I was surprised how effortlessly the lead launch towed the others. Tobey explained that both launches were powered by eight-cylinder Chrysler Imperials, capable of tremendous pulling power.

I had no idea where we were going. We sailed without lights in the predawn blackness. Tobey knew the river. He followed the channel purely by instinct, and, in all the time I sailed with him, no matter what the weather, I never saw him run off course or run aground.

I guess we'd run for about a half hour in a southerly direction when Tobey throttled down the motor and glided to a halt. He dropped the bow anchor.

"Let Kenny's boat pull up alongside," he ordered. "Loose the tow line."

I jumped to obey, but, try as I might, I could not untie the stern line. The clove hitches were pulled too tightly. I worked frantically, thoroughly embarrassed. Tobey stepped to the stern alongside me. I could see the hatchet in his hand. With one swing, he severed the tow line. I figured I was in for a bawling out, but, instead, both he and Kenny roared with laughter.

"Hey, there, Hatchet-knot!" Kenny shouted gleefully, "seems like I gotta learn you to make fast a tow line proper. Otherwise, 'stead of fishin', you'll spend all your time splicin' the ropes we have to chop up for you!"

We lay to in darkness for about a half hour. At the end of that time Tobey picked up a pinch of fine dirt and sand from the bottom of the launch and dropped it over the side. I watched as the fine particles sank slowly, drifting in a northerly direction.

"Tide's turned," Tobey remarked. "Time to go to work."

We had anchored near the east bank of the river. Captain Tobey took the net boat in tow with his launch and headed towards midstream. I stayed with Kenny in the inboard launch. One end of the seine had been secured to Kenny's launch, and, as Tobey pulled away towards the west shore, the net payed out over the stern of the net boat. Tobey's launch was soon swallowed up in the darkness. Still we could hear the rumble of the corks and leads as they rattled over the net boat's transom.

"Here's where you go to work, kid," Kenny said. "This here sloopie with all that rope piled in the stern is yours. You leave one end of the rope with me, then pull yourself along the cork line 'til you come to a strap. All the while, the line is paying out. You fasten the strap to the line this way." He showed me the particular knot used to fasten the strap in such a way that one sharp tug on its loose end would free the strap from the rope.

"Now," he continued, "you work yourself all the way around the net to Tobey's boat. Give Tobey whatever rope is left over so he can use it on the niggerhead to pull in his end of the net, same as I'll use this end. The straps will pull in the net as we haul in the rope."

The operation wasn't entirely clear to me at this point, but I got the general idea. I stepped into the sloopie, lay outstretched on its forward deck, and grabbed the moving cork line. I pulled myself along the cork line to the first strap, which I secured to the line paying out behind my boat. Soon I had lost sight of Kenny and could not yet see Tobey's launch far ahead of me. I had a long way to go, and, in the darkness, I felt completely alone. The black water slapped the sides of my sloopie, often splashing up into my face as I lay on the forward deck on my belly, doggedly pulling myself along hand over hand. My arms and shoulders ached. I was soaked through by the splashing, slapping waves, and, although I was perspiring from exertion, I was shivering with cold.

Perhaps it was the darkness all around me, or the loneliness, or the strangeness of my surroundings, or perhaps a combination of all these things that brought on a strong feeling of apprehension. My mind conjured up all sorts of catastrophies that might descend upon me at any moment. I visualized a sudden squall that could easily swamp my frail sloopie. I could see myself floundering around in the black water, weighted down by my heavy boots, rubber overalls, and rubber coat. I paused momentarily in my hand-over-hand propulsion to catch my breath and look around me. Far to the west I could see the winking yellow street lights of Jensen Beach. A mile or so to the east was the dark, forbidding mangrove swamp, inhabited only by cottonmouth moccasins, water birds, and wild creatures. To the north and south, black water stretched endlessly. I shivered again, but this time it was not from the cold.

The seine was being dragged by both launches parallel to the shore in a northerly direction with the incoming tide. When dawn finally broke, I could see Tobey's launch ahead of me, and, behind him, the great semicircle of net leading back and over to Kenny's inboard launch skirting the mangroves well inshore. The outboard launch was about five hundred yards further north than Kenny's boat.

It was daylight when I reached Tobey's boat and the now-empty net boat. Tobey grinned at me as he held firmly to the tiller bar.

"I see you're still with us," he called. "You make out all right?"

"O.K., I guess," I panted.

I threw him my bow line, and he made my sloopie fast to the side of the launch.

"Come aboard and rest," Tobey directed. "We still got a ways to go."

I tumbled, exhausted, into the bottom of the launch, too worn out to speak. Finally, when I'd regained some of my strength, I sat on the engine hatch and studied my surroundings. We had been dragging about two hours and had traveled perhaps two miles from our starting place. The sun was up now, and its warmth felt good on my tired, wet body.

"How much longer do we drag, Tobey?" I asked.

"We tie up to that big tall coconut tree up ahead," Tobey declared. "We start to turn in towards shore now."

About a half hour later, Tobey edged the bow of the launch into the shallow water on the edge of the river bank. I jumped overboard to secure the bow line to the coconut palm directly in front of us.

"Hey, kid," Tobey called after me, "remember—no hatchet knots this time!"

I waved and nodded that I understood.

Kenny had pulled his launch in to shore, parallel with us, but about fifty feet away. When both boats were secured, Tobey tied one end of a short length of net, which was piled in the third sloopie, to his launch and directed me to pole over to Kenny's boat, paying out the short net. This net was called the gate and was used to prevent the fish from escaping around the open, shore side of the semicircle.

Both Tobey and Kenny cranked up their single-cylinder, heavy-duty donkey engines. These motors, which were without mufflers, popped and crackled like strings of fire-crackers. Each was equipped with a large revolving brass winch. By wrapping around the winches the line that I had run along the cork line, both launches were able to pull in the seine. When one of the straps was brought within reach, a quick, sharp jerk separated the net from the line and the net dropped into the water alongside the net boat. My job, then, was to haul the seine back into the net boat. I first pulled in fifty feet or so of the bottom edge, or lead line, and tossed it into the stern. Next, I went forward and pulled aboard fifty feet of the cork line, which I tossed forward near the bow. Back and forth, back and forth, first to the stern to pick up the lead line, then forward to pick up the cork line. I worked as fast as I could, trying to keep up with the donkey motors, which were gradually bringing the net closer to shore.

As the circle of net became smaller, I could see the flashing sides of fish as they darted around inside. Some leaped out of water; those fortunate enough to be near the cork line when they leaped found their way to freedom over the top of the net.

I was about to drop from exhaustion when both donkey engines stopped. The net had been pulled in to shore to the point where the huge bag was only twenty feet from us. Kenny moved his launch to the outside of the bag; Tobey's boat was placed just inside. As the two men pulled up the open maw of the bag, stretching it between the two boats, I could see hundreds of pounds of fish flopping around inside the bag. Two of the sloopies were brought alongside the launches, and the job of bailing the fish out of the net with long-handled scoop nets began. I watched how it was done for a few minutes before taking up one of the nets and joining in. Only edible fish were kept. I soon learned that a third of the fish in the big bag were trash fish: stingrays, catfish, small sand or hammerhead sharks, and toadfish. These undesirable fish had to be taken out of the scoop net by hand, but before Tobey allowed me to attempt it, he showed me how it should be done.

"The stinger on a stingray is at the base of his tail," he explained. "If you don't grab him just right, he'll flip that barb into your hand quick as lightnin'. Here's what you do."

Tobey rested the handle of his scoop net on the gunwale of the boat. There was a stingray weighing about six pounds on top of the other fish in the scoop. Tobey thrust his thumb and forefinger into the stingray's eyes, curling his fingers behind the hard bone of the fish's eye sockets. With the fish held firmly in his grasp, he lifted it from the net. The thrashing tail could not touch him as he held the fish at arm's length to show me. Tobey held the fish over the side of the boat, away from the net, and let go.

"Now, catfish are even worse than stingrays, as far as you gettin' hurt is concerned," Tobey continued. "A catfish has a long, barbed dorsal fin and two barbed side fins that can really tear you up if you ain't careful. They're slimy as an eel and quick as lightnin', so watch out. Grab a catfish from the front, head on, and you'll miss gettin' the fins into your hand. They'll turn on you quick, so you got to be quicker than they are. You'll learn, probably the hard way. Get a catfish fin rammed up under your fingernail once or twice and you'll learn to handle them with care."

I nodded and joined my two partners in bailing the net. I threw the trash fish over the side and the edible fish into the sloopie nearest me. I soon realized that the other sloopie was the beer boat. Both Kenny and Tobey occasionally threw a scoopful of fish into it. I didn't contribute to the contents of the beer boat. I waited to be told to do so.

Finally, the net was empty, and, after loading the rest of the seine into the net boat, we strung out our little fleet behind Tobey's launch and headed back to Jensen Beach. Tobey cast the other launch and net boat loose near our mooring dock, and, with the fish-filled sloopies in tow, headed for the unloading dock at Pitchfords' Fish House. Kenny and I secured the net boat and launch to the net rack, then headed for Pitchfords' to meet Tobey. We met him in the usual booth and ordered beer.

"Well, boy, how do you like workin' a seine rig?" Tobey asked.

"I like it fine, Tobey," I answered, " 'cept I'm not in as tough a condition as I thought I was. My muscles feel like they're on fire."

"You're just not used to it yet, kid," Kenny remarked. "It'll take a while, but you'll toughen up. You did real good, though, your first day. Didn't he Tobey?"

"You did good," Tobey agreed. "You want to stay on the rig?"

"I sure do, Tobey. It'll take gettin' used to, like Kenny says. It's damn hard work."

"Sure it is," Kenny replied, "and some days you work just as hard and don't get enough fish to pay for the gas; ain't that so, Tobey?"

"Ya, that's the truth. Each day you don't know what you get 'til the net is picked up. One day last year, Kenny and I worked alone. We got twenty thousand pounds of bluefish out in Bessie's Cove. We worked hard that day, believe me."

"What did we do today, Tobey?" Kenny asked.

Tobey pulled a slip of paper from his pocket. "We got eight hundred twenty pounds bottom fish. They bring us ten cents a pound."

I figured it quickly to myself. The boat share was a third of eighty-two dollars, or twenty-seven. Another five for gas left fifty dollars, in round figures, to be divided three ways. I had earned sixteen dollars that day for about ten hours work. I was well satisfied.

I stayed with the seine rig, but I must admit that the evening after that first day I had serious doubts as to whether or not I'd ever become physically strong enough to stick with it. Every muscle in my body ached. I was so completely worn out I could neither eat nor relax. As I recall it now, I threw myself down on my bed and whimpered like a whipped pup.

But, like I said, I stayed with the rig. Perhaps it was because of the admiration and instant liking I felt for my partners, Captain Tobey and Kenny. Perhaps, as with most fishermen, it was because of the uncertainty of what each day might bring. The elusive pot of gold was always right out there—waiting—and, who could say? Today, or even tomorrow, might be the day we would hit that big school.

Only once during the year and a half I fished with Tobey and Kenny did we make a haul that came close to being the big bonanza all fishermen dream about.

It all started because our seine was getting completely worn out. Each time I picked up the net after several hours of dragging, I found more and bigger holes in it that needed mending. The webbing had become weakened to the point where any sunken stob or debris would rip out big chunks of the linen mesh. We found that we were unable to hold the fish we had within the circle. Mullet, especially, with their hard, bullet-like heads, were able to hit the net and pass right through it, either by stretching the mesh or by breaking it. When we had a large number of mullet in the circle, it looked like silver raindrops falling through the webbing to the outside of the circle. Our net just couldn't hold them.

One day I saw several large wooden crates piled up in the back room of Pitchfords' Fish House.

"That's new webbing for you seiners," Joe Pitchford told me in answer to my question. "My brothers and I figured it was time you got yourselves a new net."

Hanging in the new seine was a prolonged and tedious job. The leads and corks had to be cut from the old net and restrung on the new lines. This job fell to me. The new lines were stretched between two coconut palms, about a hundred feet apart, then pulled as taut as possible by means of block and tackle. Net shuttles had to be kept filled with new hanging twine, also my job, while Tobey and Kenny did the actual tying of the webbing to the cork and lead lines.

The three of us worked six days a week for about ten weeks, hanging in almost a mile of net. This included making a new bag, which was a complicated, tightly-woven piece of work which Tobey alone tackled. Of course, during those ten weeks we were "on the beach," we earned nothing, since we were not fishing. However, each Saturday morning "Doc" Pitchford, the financial administrator of the Pitchford brothers, would stop by where we were working.

"Well, Curt," he'd say, "you about ready for payday?"

"Always glad to see you, Doc, especially on Saturdays," I'd answer.

"How much you gonna need this week? Thirty? Forty? You just name it."

"Let's make it thirty-five, Doc. That'll see me through."

Doc would take a long, envelope-like leather wallet, which was fastened to his belt by a chain, from his back pocket and take out the money. He would hand me the amount I'd asked for in crisp bills, then go to Tobey and Kenny in turn and repeat the ritual. Each Saturday, though, before he left us, Doc would take a small black notebook from his shirt pocket and write down the date and the amount he had given each of us.

I believe Captain Tobey drew fifty dollars a week during the time we were on the beach. He had a wife, a teen-age daughter, and a son in high school to support.

Kenny drew the same amount as I. He lived alone in a little one-room apartment back of the hardware store. I never did figure out what he did with his money—not that it was any of my business. He, in fact all three of us, continued to get all the free beer we wanted from Pitchfords' during those weeks we were not fishing. I don't believe I ever saw Kenny sit down to a full-course meal, except when Evelyn and I invited him over to share Sunday dinner with us.

Usually, he'd munch on a box of crackers, with a beer, or a baloney sandwich, with a beer, or a piece of smoked mullet, with, of course, a beer.

We finally got our new seine hung in. There was just one more process to go through before we could be out fishing once again. We carried the new net to the river bank, where we built a wood fire beneath a fifty-five gallon drum of tar. We heated the tar almost to the boiling point. While Tobey and Kenny fed the net into the tar barrel, I stood alongside the barrel turning the crank on an old-fashioned clothes wringer, squeezing the excess tar from the dripping, steaming net. As soon as the net left the wringer, it was submerged in the salt water of the river. This process is called curing. A salt-cured net becomes as unyielding and stiff as a board, besides being preserved against rot. As I stood turning the crank of the wringer, billows of smoke from the tar barrel kept blowing in my face. I choked, coughed, and shed big, tar-flavored tears which ran down my cheeks. Tobey and Kenny seemed to get a big kick out of my predicament, but neither of them volunteered to take my place at the wringer. The following day, I learned why they were reluctant to spend any more time in the tar smoke than was absolutely necessary. My face, arms, hands—every part of my body that had been exposed to the smoke—peeled raw. My face looked like freshly ground hamburger. My eyes were swollen half shut. Actually, my face and eyes did not hurt, but I certainly did look a mess.

Two days later, we set out with our new net for the first time. The afternoon before, Joe Pitchford had admonished us:

"Now, you fellows have a brand new net, and there's no good reason why you can't bring us in some mullet. We ain't seen any good catches of mullet for a long time; you boys better bring us some tomorrow."

We left our moorings at four o'clock in the morning. The moon was just sinking below the dark sand dunes behind Jensen, and a soft mist had settled just a few feet above the black, still water. There was not a breath of wind stirring. The river stretched out like an endless, dark mirror. I stood in the forward cockpit of Tobey's launch. He stood in the stern, handling the tiller. I could not see more than six feet in front of the boat, nor could he, but he seemed to know exactly where we were going. As I looked astern, I could barely make out the net boat and Kenny's launch strung out behind us. I turned my attention forward. There was a heaviness to the air, and something else that I could not place at first, until I breathed in heavily through my nose a few times. Then it dawned on me. I smelled fish—the air reeked of fish. I couldn't understand it.

"Hey, Tobey," I yelled, sniffing loudly. "I smell fish!"

"Ah, go on," Tobey replied derisively, "that's pelican shit!"

I laughed, not convinced he was not pulling my leg.

We sailed our little fleet into Bessie's Cove and immediately went to work setting out the net. The work was routine for me now; I knew exactly what to do and when to do it with the least amount of wasted motion. I started running the line, and, as I lay prone on the sloopie's forward deck, pulling myself along hand over hand, my face was a scant foot above the surface of the water. The strong smell of fish was even more pronounced. I looked about in the predawn darkness. There was no sign of life, no splashes of leaping fish anywhere.

The sun was just rising brilliantly above the sand dunes to the east when Tobey signaled Kenny to turn in to the mangroves for a landing, while we started our sweeping circle towards the beach. Only then did we see the first signs of life within the circle of the net. Flashes of silver mullet were everywhere as they leaped high into the air, then arched gracefully back into the water.

Tobey and I secured the launch to the big coconut palm at the water's edge, and my routine of picking up the net began as the donkey engine pulled it in. Kenny was also pulling in net from his launch. As the semicircle of the mile-long seine decreased in size, the activity inside the circle increased. Mullet by the thousands flashed, darted, and leaped in a frenzy to escape the encircling net. Hundreds leaped to freedom over the top of the net; it seemed to me that not a second went by that there weren't at least a hundred fish in the air all at the same time. As the circle continued to decrease in size, I could see the net sway and surge back and forth from the combined weight of the fish charging the webbing as they sought to escape. Many of the mullet became gilled in the mesh, and this made my job of picking up net doubly hard and doubly heavy.

At long last we had the bag of the seine secured between the two launches. It was filled to capacity, even to overflowing.

"Hey, Tobey," I cried, excitedly, "how many pounds do you think we've got in there?"

Tobey was noncommittal. "Quite a several, my boy, quite a several!"

I could tell by the grin on his face that he was pleased.

We set to work bailing the fish from the pocket. It took no time at all before we had the three sloopies filled to capacity.

"Throw the net over the side," Tobey ordered. "We got to load up the net boat."

Kenny and I jumped to obey. Time was of the essence; the warmth of the water and the close confinement of the tightly packed fish would rot them all too quickly. We worked furiously, in silence, hour after hour. It seemed to me that we would never reach the bottom of the huge pocket. The net boat wallowed sluggishly in the water, her gunwales almost awash from the tremendous weight of fish we loaded into her. The forward cockpits of both launches were also filled to capacity before the net was finally empty.

I guess it was about two o'clock the following morning when we headed for the fish house. We'd been bailing fish for almost twenty hours without food and without rest. We were completely exhausted. We left the seine in the shallows, just where we had dumped it, knowing it would be safe until we were able to return to pick it up.

We found the fish house brilliantly lighted and bustling with activity when we finally reached home with our catch. We had made the five-mile trip at a snail's pace; our boats were so overloaded that any attempt at speed would surely have swamped the sloopies as well as the net boat. Even with Tobey's caution and superior skill in handling, the boats yawed dangerously during the entire trip homeward, and I felt that at any moment any one or all of them would capsize.

Doc Pitchford met us at the unloading platform.

"What do you think you're gonna do with all them fish?" he inquired, unsmiling.

"You asked for mullet, Doc," Kenny called up to him, "so we brought you mullet. Send some of those nigras down here so we can get unloaded."

"We can't use 'em," Doc replied. "We ain't got storage enough."

"What'll we do with them, Doc, eat them?" I asked sarcastically.

"Take 'em out to sea and dump 'em. We don't want 'em."

With these words, Doc turned his back and walked into his office. During our conversation with Doc, Tobey had said nothing. Now he climbed up on the platform and followed Doc into the office. He closed the door behind him.

I figure their discussion lasted a half hour. Finally Tobey emerged from the office, grim-faced and looking more tired than I'd ever seen him before. He nodded slightly to the group of Negro men sitting on fish boxes awaiting the outcome of the discussion. The men knew what to do; some jumped into the laden boats and began shoveling fish into the wire baskets that the others lowered down to them. Each basket was weighed and tallied; then the fish were dumped into the chill boxes.

Kenny and I collapsed on a pile of burlap bags in a corner, out of the way, and watched silently. We were too bone weary to speak. Tobey joined us.

"How'd we do, Skipper?" Kenny asked.

"Doc agreed to take them," Tobey replied, wearily, "but we don't get fifteen cents a pound, like he's been payin'."

"What do we get?"

"Three cents a pound for the big ones, two for the medium size, and a penny a pound for the small ones."

"Well," Kenny said philosophically, "I guess that's better than dumpin' 'em. At least we'll get rent and grub money. Shit! Come on, you guys, let's go have a beer!" He rose slowly to his feet. Tobey and I followed him to the bar in the front part of the fish house.

When the entire catch of mullet was weighed, we learned that we'd brought in thirty-seven thousand pounds! This catch should have brought us over five thousand dollars. Instead, we were compelled to settle for about seven hundred and fifty dollars. Of this, my share was around $165.00, after the boat share and gas expenses were deducted. In my eyes, I'd earned a small fortune for about twenty-four hours' work.

On payday at the end of that week, Doc met us at our usual table in Pitchfords' bar. He handed each of us a length of adding machine tape showing the total amount he had advanced us while we were on the beach hanging in the new net. A portion of this amount he deducted from the total due us for our week's catch. However, in spite of the deductions, I was able to take home more money than I'd ever earned in a week before in my life!

I've often wondered what our pay would have been that week if all those mullet had been pompano. Pompano were the money fish of that day, avidly sought after by seiners and gill netters alike. The fish house paid a higher price for them than for any other species—thirty-five cents a pound. Pompano were always in scarce supply and great demand.

Kenny was our self-appointed pompano hunter. Each morning after we'd left the dock, long before daylight, he would stand in the stern of his inboard launch shining a powerful battery-powered searchlight into the black water astern our little flotilla. For some reason, the dancing light would cause any pompano within its beam to leap from the water and skim across the waves like a flat rock thrown by a boy along a river bank. The sight of a few skimming pompano would cause Kenny to shout and wave to us excitedly, then redouble his efforts to scare up a few more with his searchlight. It often happened that, when we were ready to set out the net, we would find three or four pompano had leaped into the net boat or into one of the shallow sloopies. We never did make a really big catch of these golden-yellow beauties. I guess forty or fifty pounds was the best we ever had in one haul. Since the Indian River pompano averaged about two pounds each, this would mean that a catch of twenty or twenty-five fish was considered excellent.

It was always an accepted practice among us fishermen that we could take home for our own use any of the fish we had caught. Each of us had our preference: Tobey always chose a bluefish, Kenny was partial to sheepshead, while I preferred Spanish mackerel. It was never discussed, or even mentioned, but, as a sort of unwritten agreement, none of us ever put aside a salable pompano for our own use. By salable I mean a pompano over ten inches in length, the legal size which the fish and game commission allowed to be sold. Of course, we often found undersized pompano in the seine. These were carefully wrapped in burlap, hidden in the bow locker of the net boat, then divided equally among the three

of us when we returned to the dock. Pan-fried small pompano were about the finest fish I've ever eaten. Perhaps their
illegality added something to their flavor.

I soon learned that eating, that is, providing food for himself and his family, is of paramount importance to a Florida
fisherman. In order to survive during the lean times—those
days, and sometimes weeks, when tropical storms, red-tide
invasion, or an unexplained scarcity of fish make it imprac-
tical to go fishing—the fisherman turns to other forms of
food which the sea provides. Of course, every fisherman
keeps a supply of dried or smoked fish, mostly mullet, on
hand. Some of the old-timers even have barrels of fish packed
in rock salt as emergency rations to be used when fresh fish
are scarce.

Tobey and Kenny introduced me to the giant loggerhead,
or sea turtle, as a source of food. I believe it was during my
second week on the seine rig that we found the first giant
turtle inside the circle of the net. Both my partners were
elated as they hauled the hundred-and-fifty-pound beast
into the launch and laid it on its back. Only the Good Lord
knows how old the turtle was; its barnacle-encrusted, coral-
scarred shell gave evidence that it could have been at least a
hundred years old. As it lay on its back in the bottom of the
boat, the turtle's flippers beat the air wildly, its neck craned
backward in a desperate attempt to turn over.

"Why don't you turn him right side up, Kenny?" I asked.
"Seems like he's suffering, thrashing about like that."

"If I do, he'll die," Kenny explained. "A loggerhead is
strictly a sea turtle; he ain't built to live with anything solid

under him. If I turn him over, his own weight will press on his lungs 'til they crush, and he'll suffocate. Why, I remember one time, years ago, I rounded up a dozen big logger-heads in a little seine I was fishin' illegal, pullin' by hand. I took 'em to the fish house 'bout four o'clock in the mornin' and put 'em in an empty chill vat for safekeepin'. I planned to truck 'em to Palm Beach, come daylight, and sell 'em to the big restaurants to make soup out of. By the time I went back to the fish house, long about sunup, every one of them turtles was dead. I'd forgot to turn 'em on their backs, and they all suffocated."

When we returned to the dock that afternoon, I asked Kenny what we would do with the turtle.

"I don't like to do the butcherin'," he said. "We'll watch for a nigra to come along. He'll butcher it for us; he'll do it gladly if we promise him one of the flippers."

About ten minutes later, we saw a tall, barefooted Negro man, in his late twenties, walking along the road past our landing.

"Hey, Sam," Kenny called, "come on over here!"

The colored man immediately turned off the road and walked toward us.

"Want to butcher a turtle for us?" Kenny asked. "We'll give you a flipper for doin' it."

The Negro's face beamed. "'Why sure, Mista Kenny, I'll be glad to do it. You got a good knife?"

I handed him the six-inch sheath knife I carried on my belt. He felt its keen edge appreciatively.

"This'll do fine," he said.

He stepped into the launch where the turtle lay on its

back, still thrashing wildly. He placed one of his bare feet on the extended neck of the turtle, and I saw the bright blade of my knife flash downward.

The butchering did not take very long. Soon five chunks of meat lay on the dock. Four of the chunks resembled miniature legs of lamb; the fifth piece, the neck, looked like a length of tenderloin. Sam carefully cleaned off my knife and handed it to me, handle first. He disposed of the turtle's shell and entrails by throwing them overboard. Following that, he thoroughly cleaned up all evidence of the butchering from the bottom of the launch.

"You did a good job, Sam," Kenny said. "Help yourself to one of them flippers."

The man grinned. "'Thank you kindly, Mista Kenny. Any time you need butcherin' done, just call on me."

Sam removed his tattered shirt and carefully wrapped the turtle meat in it, then headed towards his home in the colored section south of town.

Evelyn was more than a little apprehensive when I brought home my turtle flipper and a piece of the neck meat, especially when the meat twitched and quivered as I washed it in the sink. The kids, though, were fascinated.

"How do we cook it?" Evelyn asked.

"Kenny says it's good stew meat," I explained. "It's too tough and stringy to roast."

"I'll pressure-cook it," Evelyn exclaimed brightly. "That ought to soften it up!"

For supper that evening we had the finest Hungarian goulash I have ever eaten. The cubes of meat cut from the flipper bones and neck were transformed by the pressure cooker into the tastiest, tenderest meat imaginable, almost identical to the finest cut of prime beef. The rich brown gravy, poured over egg noodles, made a meal fit for the most discriminating gourmet.

Kenny introduced us to another culinary delight which the loggerhead turtle provided. One afternoon, he came to the house carrying a brown paper bag containing about two dozen of what looked for all the world like ping-pong balls. He handed them to Evelyn.

"What in heaven's name are these?" she asked.

"Turtle eggs," Kenny replied.

Evelyn took one from the bag and examined it closely. The shell was about the thickness of a bird's egg, but was pliable, rather than brittle.

"What do I do with them?" she asked.

"You don't crack 'em like an egg; you pinch 'em open. Then you whip 'em. The more you whip 'em, the lighter and fluffier they get. Then you make an omelet or use 'em in any way you use eggs."

Kenny was right. Evelyn beat the eggs in a large bowl, and the more she beat them, the fluffier they became. Soon the bowl was filled with a golden yellow froth. That night we had pancakes for supper—pancakes made with turtle eggs. They were as light as a feather, puffed up to over an inch in height, with the consistency of a soufflé. They did not taste different from ordinary pancakes; it was their fluffy lightness that made them delicately different.

Of course, Kenny stayed to have supper with us that evening. While we were eating, he explained how he happened to have the turtle eggs.

"Me and a couple other fishermen went over to the beach

last night," he explained. "We knew it was about the right time of year for turtles to be nestin'. Sure enough, we come across a couple of females settin' over the holes in the sand they'd laid their eggs in, and we found another nest that had just been covered over with sand. The female had gone back out to sea. We dug up enough eggs for each of us, 'bout two dozen apiece."

A few weeks after the incident of the loggerhead turtle, I met my first manatee. We were just starting to take in the seine with the donkey engines when I saw a huge animal resembling a walrus rolling and diving inside the circle.

"That's a manatee; a sea cow, some people call them," Tobey explained.

"Gosh, he's big. How much do you figure he weighs, Tobey?"

"Oh, 'round half a ton, maybe."

"We gonna let him go?"

"That depends. If we don't see the game warden before we get him butchered, we'll have roast manatee for Sunday dinner."

As the circle was diminished, the giant manatee became more visible. Its movements inside the circle were leisurely, seemingly without panic. It came to the surface for air at regular intervals, then swam around slowly, just under the surface. Finally, we had it inside the bag of the net. It was much too large and heavy to pull aboard a sloopie or one of the launches, so a rope was tied around the base of its flat, dinner-plate-like tail, and it was towed to a sheltered, secluded hammock deep in the mangrove swamp on the eastern shore of the river.

It took the three of us several hours to butcher the beast.

When we finished, we had four galvanized washtubs filled with fresh meat. We kept the tubs carefully hidden until all the meat had been distributed among ourselves and our fishermen friends in Jensen.

My family and I were surprised and delighted with the flavor of the roast Evelyn fixed for supper the following evening. The meat had the flavor and texture of veal; there was absolutely no fishy taste. Manatees are vegetarians that feed exclusively on hyacinth plants, seaweed, and almost any green vegetation that grows on the river bottom or along the banks. I did find an unpleasant taste in the liver, though. It tasted strongly of agar, no doubt because of the animal's diet of seaweed.

Manatee meat was a welcome change in the diet of fishermen, and they had a unique way of preserving it. The meat was cut into strips about an inch square and a foot long. These strips were salted thoroughly, laid out in rows to dry on the tin roof of a shed or fish house, and covered with cheesecloth to protect them from insects. Every few days, each strip of meat had to be turned over so that it dried on all sides. After several weeks, the meat had the consistency of beef jerky, and it was preserved for months to come. The fishermen returned it to a palatable condition simply by boiling.

We caught and butchered a manatee on three different occasions during the time I worked with Tobey and Kenny. There were many other times when we had manatees within the circle, but they escaped. If we had a female inside the circle, we knew that we'd be unable to hold her, especially if she had one or two babies with her. If such was the case, the male manatee would not be far away, usually just outside the circle. The male would swim around outside, watching the circle of net become smaller and smaller. As the circle decreased, he would become more and more agitated. Finally, he would back away about a hundred yards, then charge the net with the speed and power of an express train. He could tear his way into the circle as if the net did not exist. Once inside, he herded his mate and offspring together, then charged the net again (always in a different place from the one he'd entered), tearing a gaping hole in the webbing through which he and his family fled. On those occasions, we lost our fresh meat and almost all our fish and had many hours of work ahead of us patching the net.

Even in those days, manatee were protected by very strict conservation laws. For that reason, we were always stealthy and secretive when we caught and butchered one. We always shared the fresh meat with other Jensen Beach fishermen; there was never a scrap wasted. To fishermen, a manatee was food, and food for themselves and their families was far more important than strict obedience to the law.

There were many instances when the words of the Jackson brothers up at St. Augustine were brought to mind. I mean when they'd said, "Fishermen take care of each other." I found that this was true with almost all fishermen, but especially with those at Jensen Beach.

I'd been on the seine rig only two or three days when, upon our return to the landing, Tobey asked me, "You drink whiskey, no?"

"Once in a while," I replied, puzzled.

"O.K. You see that little white cottage at the head of the side street over there across the road? Well, you take this nice flounder and two or three mullet over to the old lady who lives there. She'll give you a drink of whiskey."

The old lady, Mrs. Verity, answered my knock at the back door and invited me inside.

"Captain Tobey sent me over with these fish," I explained. "Can I put them in the kitchen for you?"

"That will be just fine. Put them in the sink, please."

I did as the sweet old lady directed.

"Do you work with Captain Tobey and Kenny?" she asked.

"Yes, Ma'am. I'm new on the rig."

"Isn't that nice!" Mrs. Verity said, smiling. "I've known them both ever since they came to Jensen. My late husband was a fisherman; he and Tobey worked a seine together for many years before Captain Verity passed away."

"Oh, dear me," she continued in a tone of exasperation, "I'm afraid I forgot my manners. Come, young man, you must be near worn out, not being used to such hard work. Sit a spell; I have something for you that'll take the ache out of your bones."

She scurried to a little kitchen cupboard and brought forth a nearly filled bottle of Four Roses.

"This won't hurt you, young man. Do you good, as a matter of fact."

She poured about three fingers into a juice glass and returned the bottle to the cupboard. She handed me the glass, and I drank it straight. She watched me closely as the fiery liquor brought a flush to my cheeks and tears to my eyes.

"There now," she said, smiling, "that'll do you good. It's

medicine, you know, good medicine when you're cold and tired."

We talked together for a few more minutes; then I returned to the dock. As I left, Mrs. Verity called after me, "Thank you and the other boys for the nice fish. Do come visit me again, and next time, bring your little family, if you get the chance."

Tobey and Kenny were waiting for me.

"Get your drink of whiskey?" Tobey asked.

"Sure did, Tobey. Say, what's with that nice old lady? How come we take fish to her?"

"Her husband was a fisherman," Tobey explained. "Now that he's dead, we take care of her best we can. She ain't got much money, but she's proud and won't take anything without payin' for it. She gives you a drink; that way she pays for the fish. Sometimes we clean up her yard, or whitewash a fence; always we get paid with a drink of whiskey. She won't have it no other way."

I learned that there were a few other "Widow Veritys" in Jensen. Each had had a husband who'd been a fisherman. Each was the self-imposed responsibility of the fishermen of Jensen Beach.

I can say without hesitation that the year and a half I spent working with Captain Tobey and Kenny were the most enjoyable and the most lucrative of all my commercial fishing experiences. They were dangerous years, too, because each day there was an ever-present chance of getting hurt, especially for a novice. My experience with sharks is a case in point.

Once when we were closing the circle of the net, we saw

that we'd rounded up half a dozen sharks. They were big devils, eight or ten feet long. Their dorsal fins, showing above the surface of the water, looked like toy sailboats skimming and darting within the confines of the net.

"What kind of sharks are they, Tobey?" I asked excitedly.

"Mako, most likely. Might be a hammerhead among them, too."

"How do you get them out of the net?"

"We harpoon what we can," Tobey explained. "The rest'll tear their way out through the webbing."

Tobey took his harpoon out of the rack in the net boat. It consisted of a ten-foot length of one-inch galvanized pipe with a steel-shafted, arrow-shaped blade welded into one end. Molten lead had been poured into the pipe's cavity in order to add weight. I judged the harpoon weighed about twenty-five or thirty pounds.

Tobey and Kenny poled themselves inside the circle in a sloopie. They moved the boat slowly, waiting for a shark to come within striking distance.

When a fin neared the little sloopie, Tobey stood tense, the harpoon poised, waiting for his chance. Suddenly he lunged downward. The sharp arrowhead found its mark, and Tobey held on, driving the shark to the bottom. The water was about four feet deep, and I could just make out the body of the shark pinned to the bottom by the heavy harpoon. Tobey held the fish on the bottom until it ceased to struggle. He was then able to lift the carcass into the boat. Kenny continued to pole the boat slowly as they searched for their next victim. Within an hour, they had disposed of all but one of the vicious beasts.

Meanwhile, I had jumped overboard from the launch and

was standing in front of the net gate in three feet of water watching my partners. I was fascinated by the shark hunt and forgot completely that there was only a net between me and those man-eaters. Tobey saw me.

"Hey, kid, what do you think you're doin'? Get back into that boat before one of them sharks decides he wants out. He'll charge that gate and eat you up!"

"Ah, go on, Tobey," I shouted back. "He wouldn't do that! Besides, I want to watch!"

"Do like I say," Tobey shouted sternly. "I ain't foolin'! They'll take your leg off in one bite!"

I still was not convinced. After all, there was only one shark left, a twelve-footer swimming slowly and leisurely around the inside perimeter of the circle, keeping his distance from the sloopie and the two men hunting him. The shark swam so close to the gate I could have touched him. He seemed determined to stay out of reach of the harpoon.

Suddenly a brilliant idea struck me. As slowly as that shark was swimming, I could easily slip a lasso over its tail! I took a length of half-inch manila rope from the launch, tied one end to the bow cleat, and made a running slip knot in the other end. I stood poised by the gate, waiting for the shark. He continued swimming around the perimeter of the circle. As he approached me, both his dorsal fin and his tail fin were exposed above water, giving me another bright idea. When the shark was within reach, I suddenly grabbed its tail fin, yanked up hard, then slipped the noose over it. For the next few minutes, water flew in all directions as the shark fought desperately to free himself. Kenny poled the sloopie toward me at top speed, shouting for me to "get the hell out of there."

To tell the truth, I felt more than a little chagrined, as well as elated. Here I had a beast by the tail, but what in the world could I do to stop that damn splashing? I pulled the sheath knife from my belt and attacked the shark, stabbing and slashing at the grey blur that seemed to be on all sides of me at once. I know I didn't hurt him any, and it took only one swipe of his thrashing tail to knock me flat on my back into the net gate. I can thank Kenny for pulling the shark away from me. Lord knows how I would have escaped from the net by myself. Later, when the dead beast was pulled up on the beach, Captain Tobey made it a point to pry open its jaws and show me the triple set of vicious teeth that could have severed an arm or leg in one bite. I must have turned three shades whiter when I saw those teeth. I know I made a solemn promise to myself and my partners that lying there was the first, last, and only shark I'd ever deliberately tangle with in hand-to-hand combat!

Kenny was luckier, or perhaps I should say more skillful, than I in hand-to-hand fish fighting. I found this out a few weeks after the shark incident. We had made our haul and were about ready to pick up the bag when Kenny shouted, "Hey! Look there! We got some kind of beast tangled up in the webbin'!"

I followed his pointing finger. Part of the net had become balled up and was bobbing up and down, moving rapidly first in one direction, then another.

"Guess I'll have a look-see," Kenny declared, then jumped overboard and waded to the scene of the disturbance. I could see him peering intently into the net, trying to make out what was causing the commotion. Suddenly, he dived head first beneath the water directly on top of the tangled net. He and the beast thrashed and splashed for a long minute, then Kenny struggled to his feet, his arms wrapped around something that was at least two feet taller than he.

"I got him! I got him!" he shouted as he stumbled toward us, still clutching his prize.

When he reached the launch, Kenny dumped the beast into the stern cockpit. It was a sawfish. It had the body of a seven-foot shark, but its long, flat saw extended its length another two feet. Extending from each side of the saw was a row of two-inch, evenly spaced teeth. The fish thrashed about, swinging its deadly saw from side to side.

"Well, what will you do with him, Kenny, now you got him?" Tobey asked, grinning.

"That saw ought to be worth somethin'," Kenny answered, " 'specially to the tourists. I'll peddle it in the By Jingo tonight."

The By Jingo was the only saloon in Jensen Beach that served liquor as well as beer. It was a favorite hangout for the winter tourists.

Kenny and I, still dressed in our fishing clothes and rubber boots, walked into the By Jingo together that evening. Kenny plunked the sawfish bill on the bar and ordered beer for both of us. As if on cue, Tommy, the bartender, who was behind the bar polishing glasses, exclaimed loudly, "Hi, Kenny, Curt. Whatcha got there?"

"This here's a sawfish bill," Kenny replied in a voice loud enough to carry all the way back to the john. "Don't see many sawfish in these waters, and that's a fact!"

Kenny's response brought the expected reaction. The

tourists, clad in their gaudy, multi-colored shirts, walking shorts, and knee-length socks, left their bar stools and crowded around to see for themselves. Some reached to feel the sharp, pointed teeth jutting out from the bill.

"You must have quite an outfit to land a fish like that," one exclaimed. "What'd you use, a five-hundred-yard reel? You got one of those trolling chairs and harnesses in your boat? How heavy a line do you use?"

Kenny turned slowly on his stool and looked straight at the speaker. The bored expression on his face was the result of long practice, and I had to keep my eyes riveted on my beer glass to keep from bursting out laughing.

"Hell," Kenny drawled, "we don't use none of them fancy rigs to catch sawfish. I caught him like any other Florida fisherman would of done. I jumped on his back and wrestled him 'til he got tired, then I dumped him into the boat."

The crowd laughed derisively.

"Come off it, fella; who do you think you're kidding?" Kenny's questioner asked with a sneer.

Kenny slid slowly off his stool and faced the man.

"You lookin' to call me a liar?"

The tourist looked at Kenny's barrel chest, the long, muscular arms swinging at his sides, and the apelike, unsmiling face.

" 'Course not. Must be true if you say so," he murmured and took a step backward.

I figured it was time I got into the act. "What my partner is telling you is the truth. I was with him. He jumped on top of that nine-foot sawfish in about four feet of water, wrestled him to the bottom, then came up with his arms wrapped around the fish's middle. He lugged him fifty feet to the launch and dumped him in."

The tourists seemed to take my word for it, especially when Tommy backed me up.

"That sounds just like somethin' Kenny would do. If any you guys want to rassle fer drinks, Kenny'll oblige you."

Apparently no one did; they quickly changed the subject.

"What are you gonna do with the bill?" someone asked.

"I don't know yet," Kenny replied. "It might look good hangin' up behind the bar. How about it, Tommy, wanna buy it?"

"Sure! What do you want for it?"

"What'll you gimme?"

"Five bucks?" Tommy sounded eager to buy. The tourists didn't know he was playing Kenny's game for him.

"I'll give you ten for it," interjected a tourist.

"I'll make it fifteen," said another.

An indifferent shrug of his broad shoulders was Kenny's only response.

"Tell you what, fella, I'll make it twenty. It'll look real nice in my den back home in Michigan." This came from the first tourist, the one who had shown such skepticism.

Kenny turned slowly. "O.K. It's yours. For twenty bucks."

The money and the sawfish bill quickly changed hands. Kenny and I had a few more beers, then left the By Jingo. As we were walking along the dark road towards home, Kenny handed me a ten-dollar bill.

"What's that for?" I asked.

"It's half of what I got from that hay-shaker back in the bar."

"I don't want it," I said. "It's your money; it was your fish."

"Hell, we're partners, ain't we? You was out there fishin' with me, and you went to the bar with me to sell it, so half the money is yours. Besides, I'd only drink it up anyway, and you got kids that need things."

I accepted the money, knowing that Kenny would be hurt if I didn't. He was like that.

The incident with the sawfish bill was only one of many occasions when Kenny and I got money from the tourists. Almost every day we found anywhere from one to a dozen sea horses hanging by their tails in the seine's webbing. We collected and preserved them carefully; then, once a week, usually on weekends, we'd go to the By Jingo and carefully lay them in rows on the bar. We'd get a half dollar apiece for them, except that we'd get a dollar apiece for the pregnant males. Kenny was always able to stimulate interest among the tourists by explaining that the males, rather than the females, became pregnant and gave birth. The seine often dragged up other oddities, such as small boxfish, spiney toads, and rabbit fish, all of which we unloaded for cash (or free drinks) on the tourists.

The Sunday afternoon before Thanksgiving, Kenny and I, with several other fishermen, were at the bar in the By Jingo. Soon we were joined by a fifty-year-old gill-netter named Hastings Munch, who came into the bar carrying a huge, live goose under his arm. Hastings turned the bird loose on the floor, then took a stool next to Kenny. Of course, all eyes were on the goose, who waddled about picking up crumbs, real or imaginary, from the barroom floor.

"Whatcha gonna do with the goose, Hastings?" Kenny asked.

"Why, he's gonna be our Thanksgivin' dinner."

"That so? 'Pears to me he'll die of thirst long before Thanksgivin'. Why don'tcha give him a drink?"

"Maybe you're right," Hastings acknowledged. "Here goosey, goosey! How about a beer?"

The goose waddled obediently over to Hastings and stuck his beak into the filled beer glass his owner placed on the floor. In about ten seconds the glass was empty.

"How about another?" a fisherman at the end of the bar called out, offering his glass to the bird.

"Honk! Honk!" cried the bird happily, as he waddled to his new benefactor. The second glassful of beer disappeared as quickly as the first.

"Honk!" the goose cried. This time his voice was an octave higher.

"How about a boilermaker, goosey?" another fisherman asked. "You'll be feelin' no pain, you can bet on it!"

The goose obliged by downing another beer to which a full shot of whiskey had been added.

"Honk! Honk!" This time he sounded another octave higher.

By now all the fishermen had joined in the benevolent task of slaking the poor bird's thirst. To them, he still looked thirsty, but after each beer, the goose became less and less steady on his feet. His top-heavy, wobbly walk now led him nowhere but in circles. Finally he decided he'd had enough and it was time for a nap. He lay down in the middle of the floor and promptly fell asleep.

"When are you gonna dress him out for cookin', Hastings?" Kenny asked.

"Don't rightly know."

"Now would be a good time. He'll stay asleep and won't know what's happenin' to him. Be a shame to kill him when he's sober."

"Guess you're right, Kenny. I'll do it."

Hastings picked up the sleeping goose and carried him out the back door. No one said anything for a while. Then one of the gill-netters remarked, "Y'know—that's how I wanna go. Too drunk to know what's happenin'. When you look at it, that goose was lucky. He wasn't feelin' no pain—before or after."

All along the bar I could see heads nodding in agreement.

It was during one of our visits to the By Jingo that Kenny met a young lady with whom he fell in love. Her first name was Mary, and I never did find out her last name. Everyone called her Rodeo Mary, though why, I did not have the courage to ask. Mary was a native Jensen Beach girl who had been away from home for the past five or six years. She'd been serving a term in Tahatchapee, the State prison for women. It seems that Mary had been married to a half-breed Indian construction worker, who took delight in beating up the poor girl, especially when he got drunk, which was often. The story goes that one evening Mary got pretty fed up with being slapped around by her drunken half-Indian, so she picked up an empty whiskey bottle and conked him across the head with it. He fell against the iron stove, splitting his skull open. When the police arrived, they found the husband dead, and Rodeo Mary was tried and convicted of manslaughter. She was given a sentence of from five to ten years.

Mary was out on parole when she met Kenny, and it appeared to be love at first sight. They shacked up in a fisherman's cabin on the outskirts of town and were apparently as happy together as two clams on a mud flat. Kenny got some good home cooking for a change, spent at least four out of seven evenings at home, and seemed to thrive on his new domestic arrangement. Rodeo Mary seemed completely content. She took good care of Kenny, kept him relatively sober, and didn't fight with him very much.

It was about time Kenny got a break. He had been alone for a long time, which meant that for many years he had never really had a home. He'd been married once up in North Carolina, he told me, but the marriage didn't last very long. His wife Elsie was a little bit of a thing, about four feet ten, and weighed only about eighty pounds soaking wet. It seems she'd come from a circus background; both her parents worked with a small traveling show, and so had Elsie, before she and Kenny got married. Elsie was a skilled performer. She was a knife thrower. According to Kenny, that was the undoing of their marriage. Evidently, Elsie never forgot her profession, and one night, during a knock-down, drag-out argument, Kenny picked up his hat and headed for the door. Just when he had his hand on the knob—WHAP!—a ten-inch carving knife stuck quivering in the door frame not an inch from Kenny's ear!

"I wasn't no fool," Kenny concluded when he told me the story. "I went through that door like it wasn't there and just kept goin'. I think I ran all the way from North Carolina to Jensen Beach without even stoppin' to catch my breath!"

Potential dangers surrounded us out there on the seemingly peaceful Indian River, and my partner had an experience that, on the surface, seems to be an amusing tale but could have been fatal to poor Kenny. It happened before I joined the seine rig, during the time when old Pete Donnerson was running the inshore launch and Kenny was doing my job, running the line.

It was one of those quiet, pitch-black, predawn mornings. Captain Tobey had run out the net and was towing his end of it far out in midstream. Pete was hugging the shore, towing the inshore end parallel with Tobey. Kenny lay flat on his belly on the bow of his sloopie, pulling himself along hand over hand, tying the mile-long rope to the net straps. He had gotten about halfway around the net, groping along in the blackness, when suddenly a giant "thing" came hurtling out of the water not two feet from the sloopie. It shot upward ten feet in the air, then came down, landing in the middle of Kenny's back and knocking him onto the floor of the boat, which was lucky for him. Had he been knocked overboard, he probably would have drowned. The weight of his boots, rubber pants, and coat would have pulled him under, and besides, the force and weight of the creature falling on him had knocked out his wind.

As Kenny told it:

"I landed on my back in the bottom of the sloopie with that monster on top of me. I couldn't see what it was; it kept whappin' me and stompin' me so's I had to keep my arms over my face to keep it from knockin' my head off. I couldn't fight back; I didn't know where in hell I was supposed to hit it. Besides, its weight on top of me wouldn't let me breathe. I guess it weighed as much as a full-grown man."

The fight must have lasted several minutes and then ended as suddenly as it had begun. The creature stomped Kenny a few extra licks for good measure, then flopped overboard.

Of course, the other fishermen found Kenny's story pretty hard to swallow, but he sure had the bruises all over his body to prove it. There was one other piece of evidence that showed it wasn't just "Old Budweiser" talking. The bottom of Kenny's sloopie was covered with large, silvery scales about the diameter of a beer can. Near as they could figure out, Kenny had been jumped by a gigantic tarpon, which must have weighed between a hundred and fifty and two hundred pounds.

After he had recovered sufficiently from the beating, Kenny carefully gathered up all those scales and took them, a handful at a time, to the By Jingo. He swapped them with the tourists for free drinks and, as a result, wasn't worth a tinker's damn on the seine rig for the next two weeks.

I saw the danger of the stingray's barb demonstrated one day when we'd completed our haul and were pulling in the net. Usually it was my job to wade from one launch to the other with the net gate, but this time Tobey chose to carry the gate himself. He had waded through the waist-deep water about halfway to Kenny's launch when he suddenly stumbled.

"Aaah!" he cried hoarsely and pulled his left leg from the water. I could see a large stingray dangling from his rubber waders. Tobey had apparently stepped on or near it, and the ray had thrust its barbed tail through the waders and into the calf of his leg. I saw him reach down and savagely yank out the barb, then hurl the fish far into the mangroves. Kenny immediately jumped overboard and hastened to Tobey's side. Supporting the captain's weight as best he could, he guided him back to the launch. I knew Tobey was in severe pain. His face was ashen and contorted, and he moaned softly as we helped him out of his water-filled waders. I looked at Kenny.

"What do we do now?"

"Nothin' much we can do out here," Kenny replied. "He's in real bad pain. Maybe we ought to take him ashore."

Tobey overheard Kenny's suggestion.

"No! We stay and pick up the net. Help me get on the stern deck; then start the motor."

We guided him to the stern deck, where he sat with his bare legs dangling overboard. His injured left leg hung next to the exhaust pipe. When the motor started, the exhaust pipe spewed boiling-hot water which had circulated through the motor's cooling system. Tobey thrust his left leg into the rush of two-hundred-degree water. He clenched his teeth, and I saw the tears well up in his eyes. He said nothing, but I knew the pain must have been unbearable. I turned my face away, not wishing to see his agony.

Somehow we completed the haul that day, but only because Tobey had ordered us to do so. Kenny and I worked
as fast as we could; nevertheless, it was three hours later before we finally headed home. It was almost a week before
Tobey was able to return to the rig. Even then, he still
limped painfully and stood on his leg as little as possible. He
showed me the ugly red wound left by the stingray barb. It
had torn a hole in his leg almost an inch in diameter and
must have gone through to the bone.

"It's them little needle-sharp barbs, like a double row of
fishhooks on the sides of the main barb, that does the damage," he explained. "They go in easy, but when you pull
them out they tear a hole like you see there. Besides, they got
some kind of poison in them that the stingray uses to kill
small fish with. That's why I held my leg under the exhaust
pipe. The hot water helps draw out the pain as well as the
poison."

"What kind of medicine did you use to heal it, Tobey? It
looks nice and clean and doesn't seem to be infected."

"Only thing I ever use is the juice of the aloe plant,"
Tobey explained. "It grows all around here; I grow aloe in
my front yard. Whenever I get cut, or catfish finned, or even
stingray hit, I cut a stalk from the aloe plant and make a
poultice out of the juice. Best medicine in the world! All the
fishermen keep plenty of aloe growing around their houses."

Apparently, the homegrown remedy did its job. Tobey's
wound did heal, eventually, leaving only a small white scar.

In spite of the daily perils, the long hours of hard work,
and the continual battle against wind, weather, and tides, I

was sorry to see our seining days ended. It was the County Commissioners of Martin County who put us out of business. They passed an ordinance outlawing the use of seines in the Indian River. Indirectly, it was the tourists, with the help of certain business interests, who insisted that such a law be passed.

For years, the little village of Jensen Beach had been a mecca for winter visitors. It was quiet, peaceful, off the beaten path, an ideal place for the tired Northerner to relax for a few months without having to spend a small fortune, as would have been the case in Miami or Palm Beach.

The fishing at Jensen was excellent. There was an old wooden bridge spanning the river, and fishing from this drawbridge was about the only sporting diversion the town afforded. There was a statute on the books that prohibited dragging seines within a mile of the bridge in either direction, and all the seine crews conscientiously abided by that law. However, the "sport" fishermen insisted that the seiners were taking all the fish out of the river, leaving none for them. You see, as "sports," they fished from the bridge for trout, bluefish, mackerel, and various species of bottom fish. After each day's fishing, they would take their catch to the fish house at the foot of the bridge and sell them. I have often seen a tourist return to the bridge day after day, catching enough fish to pay all his vacation expenses and more besides. Yet they resented and despised us who earned our livelihood, supported our families, and contributed to the community by paying taxes through our commercial fishing.

Apparently, the hue and cry against commercial fishing was strong enough to influence the county commissioners. It seems ironic that the two commissioners who led the fight to abolish seining had themselves been seiners before they became politicians, as had their fathers before them.

The Pitchford brothers took the news of the abolition of seining quite stoically. Doc Pitchford made contact with a representative of the Dominican Republic to negotiate a contract whereby our seine rig would be authorized to fish in the waters of the Dominican Republic and supply that island with fish. It was an exciting idea; I believe I would have gone along with it if Captain Tobey and Kenny had accepted Doc's offer to operate the seine in foreign waters. However, Tobey refused to go, and so did Kenny.

The Pitchford brothers bought a surplus Navy PT boat to transport our net boat, launches, and sloopies to the Dominican Republic. The net boat and sloopies were hoisted aboard and lashed to the deck of the PT boat, while the two launches were towed astern. Ordinarily, one would consider the trip from Florida to the Island of Hispaniola a comparatively simple one. It was not so in this case. The PT boat was caught in mid-ocean by a severe squall and had to fight for its life. Both launches were swamped by the giant waves and had to be cut loose. The net boat broke its mooring and was washed overboard. The destruction of our seine rig was complete, and it was never rebuilt.

# 9 ~ Blue Crabs and Wire Traps

**B**OTH KENNY AND CAPTAIN TOBEY continued to fish in the Indian River, but now they worked independently, each with his own gill net. I did not ask to team up with either of them; I realized that gill netting was strictly a one-man operation. Although I was certain that either of my former partners would have taken me with him, I felt it would have been an imposition to ask that he share his livelihood with me. I felt lost without the seine rig, but I was determined that somehow I'd continue fishing for a living. I knew that gill netting was not the answer; I just was not experienced enough.

On the riverfront in Salerno, just a few hundred feet from Pitchford's #2 fish house, was a crab processing plant. There, live blue-claw crabs were boiled and the meat extracted and refrigerated in tins to be sold later as fresh crab meat to restaurants in the resort cities along Florida's Gold Coast. When I visited the crab house looking for work, I was told by Mr. Hawkins, the owner, that one of his crabbers was leaving, and that a boat, plus a hundred and fifty traps, were at my disposal if I cared to become a crabber. I jumped at the chance. Here was an opportunity to make a living in an entirely new way, working independently on the river that I'd come to know and love dearly.

Running a string of crab traps cannot be considered hard work; not when you compare it with seining. The trap is a cube of turkey wire, measuring roughly two feet in all directions, with funnels at the bottom on all four sides through which the crabs enter, a bait well in the center, and a door in the top through which the trap is emptied and baited. A six- to ten-foot length of ⅜-inch manila rope is tied to one of the top corners of the trap, and on the other end of the rope is attached almost anything that floats—a coconut, a plastic bleach bottle, or a few net corks. These floats are the markers indicating the location of the trap. Usually, each crabber has some distinctive mark by which to identify his traps.

Mr. Hawkins introduced me to Ben, the crabber whose outfit I was taking over. Ben was a pleasant, likable man, about my own age, who seemed pleased that I would continue running the traps he had set out.

"It ain't hard to make a livin' runnin' a crab line," he told me. "With a hundred and fifty traps, you should bring in around three to four hundred pounds a day. The crab house pays five cents a pound, live weight. Out of that you gotta buy bait and gasoline."

"What kind of bait do I use?" I asked.

"Almost any trash fish. Jacks are best 'cause they're so bloody, but catfish, ladyfish, and sea robins are all good bait. Any kind of bait fish costs you a penny a pound, and you'll use about a hundred pounds a day."

The following morning I met Ben at the crab house at daybreak. He led me to the boat that I'd be using in my new venture. It was a sixteen-foot sloopie, equipped with a little five-horsepower, air-cooled motor.

"You don't have to worry about burnin' a lot of gas," he explained. "You can run this thing on less'n a gallon a day."

We left the crab house and an hour later sighted the buoy marking the start of Ben's trapline. He throttled down the motor, swung in close to the bobbing coconut, then deftly snagged it with a gaff hook. The trap was pulled aboard, and I could see six large blue-claw crabs scrambling frantically around inside the wire trap. When Ben maneuvered the boat in a big circle, I emptied the crabs into one of the galvanized garbage cans we had aboard, then rebaited the trap with a chunk of catfish. By the time I was ready to drop the trap back overboard, Ben had completed the slow circle, and we were back to the approximate spot where the trap had been.

"You try to keep a straight line of traps," Ben explained, "in case you get caught out here in a fog, or in rough water, or in heavy rain. It's easier to find the next trap if they're in a straight line."

We continued on to the next trap, where we followed the same procedure as before. Then on to the next, and the next. Ben had laid out his trapline so that half the traps were on one side of the river, the other half along the opposite shore. In this way, we were heading homeward as we picked up the last seventy-five traps.

All in all, it was a good day. We'd gotten almost five hundred pounds of crabs, to a gross worth of about twenty-five dollars, and we were back in Salerno by two in the afternoon. I was pleased with the potential I could see in crabbing. I was sure there was a good living to be made; surely the abundance of crabs made the prognosis favorable. I looked forward to taking over the line the following morning.

I ran my traplines five days a week; sometimes, during the long hours of daylight in summer, I ran the traps twice a day, in the early morning and late evening. To me, it wasn't work; it was fun. I must admit though, it wasn't all "beer and skittles." There were days when drenching squalls came up, and I'd be soaked to the skin. As I'd head for home, cold, wet, and hungry, the five-mile journey back to the crab house seemed like a hundred, and my little air-cooled motor seemed to be pushing backward instead of forward. The sloopie just wasn't built for rough weather. The wind blew hard and cold from the north during the winter months, churning the river into froth-crested three- or four-foot waves. At such times, my boat pounded its flat bottom with a tooth-jarring thud after each wave rolled under it, leaving her hanging in midair for that second or two before she slapped down hard into the next trough. The sloopie had no more freeboard than a rowboat, and about as much grace to her lines. Whenever I took a pounding such as I've described, I got soaked by every whitecap that the wind carried over her side and dumped into my lap. Luckily, I always carried a bailing bucket, and used it, too, to keep my sloopie afloat. It was days like that when the trapline seemed endless and the journey home an eternity. I wondered if it was such times that Father had in mind when he spoke of a wet butt.

Perhaps it just wasn't in the cards that my good fortune should last for any substantial length of time. After about eight months of running my crab lines, I was driven out of business, not by a shortage of crabs, nor by an accident, but by thieves.

I did not notice my traps disappearing at first, the loss was so gradual; but eventually, when I'd completed the line a half hour or so ahead of schedule, and when the last or the first trap was not opposite a familiar landmark on the river bank, I became suspicious and decided to count. I found that I had only a hundred and twenty-odd traps instead of a hundred and fifty. The day after I'd counted the traps, I counted again. Now I had a hundred and twenty.

When I returned to the crab house that evening, I mentioned it to Mr. Hawkins.

"We ain't had no bad storm to blow 'em off course," he said. " 'Pears to me somebody's liftin' 'em."

I agreed. "Guess I'll go back there tonight," I said. "Maybe I can catch whoever's doing it."

"Ain't no stranger bringin' crabs here to my house," Hawkins stated. "Only you and my regular boys, and ain't none of them bringin' more than their average. Besides, ain't no Florida fisherman'd steal traps outa someone else's line. Must be a newcomer, and he must be sellin' to a house up in Fort Pierce."

That evening after dark, I returned to the area where my traps were strung out in single file along the edge of the channel. I kept my sloopie's motor throttled down and hugged the river banks, keeping in the shadows. I stopped the motor when I was opposite the middle of the line, then dropped anchor to watch and wait. I peered out into the darkness and could see five or six of the buoys in the string nearest me, but was unable to see any of the traps along the opposite shore. I listened intently for the sound of a boat motor, but heard nothing except the rustle of the palm fronds along the river bank and the gentle lapping of the water against the side of the boat.

I stayed there at anchor all night, watching, listening,

straining my eyes and ears to catch some sign that I was not alone on the river. I saw and heard nothing. It was an interminable, lonely night, and when day finally broke, I aroused from my lethargic stupor and looked around me. The string of traps on my side of the river seemed to be intact. There were no boats in sight. I drank the last of the cold coffee in my thermos, stretched my cramped, aching muscles, then started the motor and headed for the opposite river bank.

I could see my traps clearly, or at least what was left of them. I counted six buoys. I'd lost about fifty traps overnight. Heartsick and completely exhausted, I returned to Salerno.

"That's a tough break, Curt," Mr. Hawkins said kindly. "You sure you didn't see anything, or hear a motor launch, or nothin'?"

"Not a sign, not a sound all night long. Whoever stole those traps must have had sail or else poled their way along. Those traps just disappeared into thin air."

"Well, I can't afford to put out more traps if they're gonna be stolen," Hawkins stated flatly. "Suppose you bring in the rest today and sit tight till we clear up this thievin'. I'll notify the game warden, then I'll contact the other crab houses along the river to see if they know anything."

About a week later, I returned to Salerno. Mr. Hawkins was not encouraging.

"You ain't the only one losin' traps to that thief," he told me. "Every house along the river is havin' the same trouble, and don't nobody know who's behind it. Near as we can figure, whoever's pickin' up them traps is not settin' 'em here. We figure he's truckin' 'em fifty, maybe a hundred miles away. He sure ain't in this county, or St. Lucie or Palm Beach counties either. If he was, we'd know it. Whoever the thievin' bastard is, he's put you and a lotta other crabbers out of business. I even gotta go over to the West Coast to buy my crabs, iff'n I wanna keep my house runnin'. We'll catch up with him sooner or later. When we do, I'll let you know."

What could I say? I didn't have much faith in the thief being caught—not in the near future, anyway. He was a slick one, I had to admit—far too slick to be caught in a hurry. Meanwhile, I was out of a job.

"Well, little man, what next?" I asked myself.

# 10 ~ Go West, Young Man

I AM QUITE CERTAIN Horace Greeley did not have the West Coast of Florida in mind when he gave the admonition that heads this chapter. Nonetheless, to me, west could only mean the other side of the Florida Peninsula, and that is where I eventually continued my life as a Florida fisherman.

I got the idea of going to the Gulf Coast from some of the men at the fish house in Fort Pierce. I'd gone there looking for work, not on one of the boats, necessarily, but in the fish house, icing down and loading fish. I needed a job; my funds were about gone. I didn't have any luck; the fishermen had all the hands they needed. I hung around awhile, watching some Negroes icing down a species of fish with which I wasn't familiar.

"What kind of fish are those?" I asked. "Seems like we never got them in the seine."

"Them's grouper, Suh," volunteered one of the men. "Grouper and some red snapper."

"They catch them here in the river?"

"No, Suh, they's caught way offshore, 'bout a hundred miles out in the ocean."

"Wow!" I exclaimed. "How deep do they fish out there?"

"Thirty fathom, maybe."

"They got nets that'll fish that deep?"

The Negro man smiled at my ignorance.

"No, Suh, they cain't use no nets out there. They fish with hand lines."

I was fascinated. "How long do they stay out?"

"Usual 'bout a week. Sometimes they fills the fish box in five days, or they runs outta ice; then they comes in sooner."

"Know if any of the grouper boats needs an extra hand?"

"No, Suh, cain't say. We got three boats what fishes outta here regular, and far's I know, they got their steady crews. You might ask the skipper of that boat we just unloaded. He's aboard, I reckon."

I stepped aboard the fishing boat tied up at the unloading dock. At the sound of my step, a middle-aged man came from the cabin.

"I came up here from Jensen looking for work. Thought you might be needing an extra fisherman."

"You ever do any fishin'?"

I told him of my experience, from charter boats, to shrimpers, to seine rigs, to crab traps.

"Sounds like you been around a little. Ever fish grouper?"

I admitted that I had not.

"Well, ain't too much different from any other kind of fishin', 'cept we use hand lines. I just ain't got room for another hand. I got two boys now that fish with me regular, providin' we can get out."

"Don't you get out to fish all the time?"

"Hell, no, much as we'd like to. That Atlantic Ocean is a mean son of a bitch, especially a hundred miles out where the fish are. This ain't no ocean liner; we gotta watch the weather mighty careful. There are more bad days out there than good, 'specially in the fall and winter months. We're lucky to get out two times a month right through April. Now, you take the West Coast. The grouper and snapper boats can fish the Gulf of Mexico twelve months a year—ten, anyway. Sometimes I got half a mind to take my boats to fish over there, 'stead of here."

"If you ever decide to go to the West Coast, what town would you fish out of?" I asked.

"Don't make too much difference. They fish grouper from Naples all the way up to Panama City in the Panhandle. I kinda like Sarasota, though. Guess that's where I'd end up."

"Well, Skipper," I said in leaving, "thanks for the information. Who knows, we might meet again someday in Sarasota."

"Good luck, kid," the captain replied, smiling. "Keep your bilges dry."

It took less than the driving time between Fort Pierce and Jensen Beach for me to make up my mind. I'd go to Sarasota just as soon as possible; that is, as soon as I could convince Evelyn that it was the right thing to do. When I spoke of it that evening, I interpreted her comment of "Well, here we go again" to mean that she was all for it. We agreed that she and the kids would remain in Jensen. When I'd gotten a job and found a suitable place for them to live, I would drive back to get them.

I left the following morning, my duffle bag filled with clothes, my heart filled with hope and great expectations. My restless feet and my equally restless spirit were on the move again, and I was happy. New adventures? New dangers? New disappointments? Who cared? I was on my way to find the other end of that elusive rainbow.

Sarasota, in 1951, was a nice little city about the size of

Fort Pierce, but actually not much different from the many other fishing towns I'd been in. It had the usual number of hotels and bars, and the usual city pier where pleasure boats rubbed fenders with drab-looking fishing boats. I rented a room in one of the less expensive hotels, then set out on foot to explore the waterfront.

I found only two boats which, from their appearance, I took to be grouper boats. Both were about forty feet in length, distinguishable as grouper boats by the huge wooden fish boxes that occupied most of their stern cockpits. I went aboard both of them but found them deserted. I left the docks and walked to the nearest waterfront bar.

After my eyes had become accustomed to the dimness, I took a stool next to two young men who had the appearance of being fishermen—you know, knee-high rubber boots, faded dungarees, and bare torsos burned the color of rich chestnut. One of them wore a battered, once-white, captain's cap. I ordered a beer and sat quietly, listening.

"What did we weigh in this trip, Skip?" the bareheaded one inquired of his companion.

"A little over five thousand pounds," the skipper replied. " 'Bout half of it was snapper."

"Hey there, how about that?" the other shouted. "Guess we're doin' O.K., eh Skip?"

The captain grinned. "Not bad, Paul. Reckon y'all can buy your kids them new school outfits now."

"Yeh, how about that! Might even get Mary that new dress she saw down in Belk's window. Might even have enough left for a few rounds of beer."

The skipper did not feel it necessary to reply. Both men

grinned happily and sipped their beer. While there was a lull in their conversation, I touched the skipper's arm.

"I don't mean to butt in," I said apologetically, "but I couldn't help hearing you and your partner talking. I'm a commercial fisherman from over on the East Coast, and I came over here to see if I can find a berth on a grouper boat. Name's Curt."

"Glad to know you, Curt. My name's Bill Travis; this here's Paul, my partner."

We shook hands all around. I noticed both men were looking me over carefully. Paul looked especially hard at my hands.

"What kind of fishin' you been doin', Curt?" Captain Bill asked.

I told him.

"Well, if you think you wanna fish handline, then that's what you oughta do."

"Any chance of sailing with you fellas?"

"We're a two-man boat, same as most of the Gulf fishermen. We're full up, and so are the other crews we know here in Sarasota. Sorry—wish we could take you on."

He was silent for a few moments, then addressed me again.

"Tell you what, Curt; why don't you try Nokomis? That's a little fishin' town about fifteen miles south of here. They got a fish house there that's always cryin' for fishermen. They got a fleet of over twenty boats. There's sure to be a berth on one of them."

"Thanks, Capt'n Bill. I appreciate the help. I'll drive down there tomorrow."

The following day was Sunday, but I chose to drive to

Nokomis anyway. I figured the fish house might be closed, but I'd have a chance to look the situation over.

I was wrong about the fish house being closed. I arrived there shortly after noon and found it bustling with activity. The huge ice-crushing machine was going full blast, chewing up the three-hundred-pound cakes of ice being fed into its wide maw and spitting out finely crushed ice from the other end. The chopped ice, looking like fine hail, was being shoveled into the huge fish box of the boat tied securely to the loading platform. There were four men working at the ice machine. Two others were scurrying back and forth to the boat, carrying boxes of groceries and tubs of salted bait. Another dozen lounged on bundles of burlap or overturned fish boxes, apparently waiting their turn to load. I could make out about ten boats lined up in both directions from the loading dock.

With all that activity going on, I figured it would be best if I found a corner somewhere out of the way and just watched. There was a blackboard fastened to the wall alongside a small, glass-enclosed office. On the board was written: Grouper—10¢. Red Snapper—20¢. I guessed that the fish house had written the going wholesale price on the board for the benefit of the fishermen. Each time a boat, or fleet of boats, was preparing to sail, the price they would receive for their catch was posted before sailing time. That way, if the market dropped, the fishermen could hold the fish house to the price posted. By the same token, any rise in prices would not affect the fisherman until his next trip.

I guess I'd been sitting alone in my corner for about an hour when I was approached by a tall, slender man in his late forties. From his appearance, and the fact that he carried a clipboard and pencil with him, I deduced he was the fish house manager. I noticed he wore a hearing aid in his ear, with the control mechanism protruding from his shirt pocket.

"Are you a fisherman?" he inquired.

"Yes, I am."

"Want to fish?" He looked me over carefully.

"I'd sure like to," I replied.

"Want to fish on a sober boat?" He said this in low tones.

"I'm not a drunk, if that's what you mean. I don't believe in mixing salt water and alcohol—especially out there." I pointed in the general direction of the Gulf.

"My brother-in-law needs a striker. That's him standin' over there—he owns the *Clara*. He's deaf and dumb. You want to go fishin' this afternoon?"

I hesitated for a few seconds, studying the man the manager had pointed out. I saw a young, tall, raw-boned man in his early twenties lounging against a pile of fish boxes, apparently waiting his turn to load up. He stood apart from the others, oblivious to the noise and snatches of conversation and laughter going on around him.

"Call him over; I'd like to meet your brother-in-law."

"The manager stomped loudly on the wooden floor. The vibrations through the planking reached the deaf man, and he looked in our direction. Immediately there was a short conversation in sign language between the two men. The boy nodded and walked over to where we stood.

"This is Captain George Reynolds," the manager said. "What's your name?"

"I'm Curt," I replied. "Glad to know you, George." I extended my hand.

He shook my hand and smiled, glancing quickly at the manager, who was, I believe, spelling out my name in sign language.

There followed a sign conversation between the two men that lasted several minutes. I watched, fascinated, trying to get some inkling of what they were talking about. It was no use—their fingers, hands, and facial expressions changed so rapidly I could not possibly keep up with them. Finally, the manager, whose name I learned later was Ted, turned to me.

"George says he'll give you a try. If you work hard and do good handlin' the boat, you get half the net profit. If you don't—well, we'll see when you come back. Go with George—he'll show you his boat."

We walked along the string of boats tied to the loading dock until we came to the *Clara.* My first impression, which I did not say out loud, was "My God—what a tub!"

The *Clara* was twenty-seven feet long, with an eight-foot beam and a round bottom. There was a raised-deck cabin forward; illumination and air were supplied to the cabin by three portholes in each side. The cabin was about ten feet long; there was no forward deck except the cabin roof. The stern deck was narrow, only about two feet wide. The rest of the boat was stern cockpit. Forward in the cockpit, up against the cabin bulkhead, aft of a sloping windshield, was the wheel, a pilot's chair, and a box compass. There was a flush hatch cover in the floor that hid the bilge and the six-cylinder Chrysler Crown motor. All of the remaining cockpit area was taken up by a huge fish box. The box was at least ten feet long, five feet wide, and five feet high. There was only a narrow space left on each side for walking, and the same narrow walkway between the back end of the box and the stern deck. The *Clara* was old, filthy, neglected, and, I learned later, leaked like a sieve. So this was to be my home away from home, a hundred-odd miles out in the Gulf, for the next week! I must have had rocks in my head to trust this tired, battered, worm-eaten hulk any further than the inlet, but I'd said I'd go, and I wouldn't back down now.

When I stepped on the *Clara*'s gunwale, she listed perceptibly, rolling on her round bottom like a waterlogged duck. I explored the forward cabin. It was damp and musty, in spite of the open portholes. There were two bunks built into the sides. (I was back to my potato bin, but at least these had mattresses of sorts.) There was a bottled gas stove, a sink with a hand pump, and food storage cupboards. A toilet stood exposed at the forward end of the cabin. I learned later that the toilet was strictly ornamental; it didn't work, and hadn't worked for over a year. On the wall alongside the toilet was the boat registration in a small black frame. Next to it hung a barometer.

I returned to the loading platform and stood with Captain George awaiting our turn to load up. George carried a little pad and a pencil with him constantly; it was the only way we could communicate.

"What do you think of my boat?" he wrote.

"It's a nice boat," I lied.

"If you have clothes and gear in your car, bring them aboard now."

It was fortunate that I'd not unpacked my gear at the hotel. I took aboard the *Clara* those things that I thought I'd need: my foul weather gear, rubber boots, an extra pair of work pants, shirts, and a change of socks. I took no toilet articles. I wasn't figuring on shaving.

After I'd stowed my gear as best I could in the musty cabin, I returned to the loading platform. George was nowhere in sight, and, in answer to my inquiry, Ted said, "George went to get the groceries. He'll be back before it's your turn to ice up."

It was about an hour later when my new skipper returned in a battered Chevy pickup. I helped him carry the cardboard boxes of groceries aboard the *Clara* and stow them in the dingy cupboards in the tiny galley. He'd bought plenty of food, I was glad to see; apparently he liked to eat well, judging by the steaks, chops, hamburger, and hot dogs we stowed away. The boxes also contained plenty of cigarettes and several boxes of candy bars, cookies, and the like.

I guess it was around 4 P.M. when our turn to ice up finally came. I stood at the shoot and shoveled the finely chopped ice into the *Clara*'s fish box as George fed the huge cakes into the crusher. We'd loaded over a ton before the box was filled to the brim. George indicated to me that I was to put our perishables—meat, milk, and butter—into the fish box on top of the ice. While I was carrying out his order, George started the motor and prepared to cast off.

The *Clara* wallowed sluggishly as we pulled away from the platform and slowly made our way across the wide canal to a small group of houses on the opposite side. They were inexpensive, neat little cottages, freshly painted white, and appeared to be immaculately kept. It was in one of them that George lived with his sister and her husband, Ted. All of the family were deaf to some degree. I learned later that all the cottages in that group were occupied by deaf families, all the families were related to one another, and all the menfolk of the community were fishermen.

We moored at the small dock in front of the cottages, and George stepped ashore after indicating to me to remain aboard. He was gone about half an hour. Upon his return, he carried a napkin-covered tray, which he handed to me. I was pretty hungry by that time, and the supper he'd brought for me looked mighty appetizing. I dined regally on fried fillet of red snapper, boiled potatoes sprinkled with finely chopped parsley, fresh string beans, and, for dessert, homemade chocolate cake and coffee. When I'd finished every scrap, I guess my wide, satisfied grin showed George how much I'd enjoyed it. I wrote on his pad: "Thank your sister for me; it was delicious."

He grinned and nodded, then returned to the house with the empty tray. He was back aboard the *Clara* in a matter of minutes. He started the motor again, but we did not shove off immediately. George indicated for me to stand beside him at the open engine hatch cover. He throttled the motor down as slow as it would go, then cupped his ear, indicating that he wanted me to listen to the rhythm of the pulsating motor. I listened attentively to the steady tick-tick-ticking of the valves and tried to match its rhythm with my hands as though I were conducting an orchestra. George looked at my face and raised his eyebrows. I gave him the O.K. sign; the motor sounded perfectly tuned.

We shoved off then. It was about six o'clock.

The *Clara* made her way through the winding channels to the Nokomis Inlet. Navigating the inlet was no problem. It was a straight, wide, deep channel, hemmed in on both sides by sturdy rock and concrete jetties. Except for a slight rolling ground swell, it was difficult to tell that we'd left the bay and were out into the Gulf of Mexico.

I estimated our speed at between eight and ten knots. The *Clara* seemed to handle well; the added weight of the ice we'd taken aboard kept her from rolling too noticeably. I noted that the box compass forward of the wheel indicated we were heading due west.

"How long do we sail before we reach the fishing grounds?" I wrote.

George indicated on his fingers ten or twelve hours.

That would put us offshore about a hundred miles.

"Do we continue sailing due west?" I wrote.

George wrote back, "We are not sailing west—we are sailing southwest by west. The compass is wrong—sometimes it is ten or fifteen degrees wrong. It all depends."

Depends on what? I wondered.

"How do you find your way back home with a compass that doesn't work right?" I wrote.

George shrugged and smiled at me.

"We do, somehow," he wrote. "Do you worry?"

I shook my head.

We continued on a steady course. Now the ground swell was more pronounced, and the *Clara* rose and fell sluggishly as we plodded on. I looked astern. We were well out of sight of land.

Darkness fell more suddenly than I thought it should have,

perhaps because there were no street lights coming on at dusk and no houses illuminated by porch lights. There were no lights anywhere—the darkness was like a blanket that closed us in, suddenly and completely on all sides.

George turned on a tiny bulb that illuminated the compass in front of him. Even this tiny light seemed to brighten up the entire cockpit, but, at the same time, it accentuated the darkness that I could feel just outside.

I offered to spell George at the wheel, but he declined, indicating to me to get some sleep. He would awaken me in a few hours. I obediently climbed into one of the bunks below deck, fully clothed. I fell asleep soon after my head hit the pillow.

George shook me awake around midnight. When I joined him at the wheel, he indicated the compass and bid me hold the course steady in the "westerly" direction the compass needle pointed. He assigned me another task, which I must not fail to carry out. Once every hour I had to man the hand bilge pump, which was secured to the port bulkhead alongside the wheel. He lifted the floor hatch cover, and I could hear the water sloshing around in the bilge. When I shone a flashlight down into the blackness of the hold, I could see that the water was almost a foot deep. It had almost reached the motor mounts. George closed the hatch, and I nodded that I understood what I was expected to do.

George went below to sleep, and I maintained my lonely vigil at the wheel—and the bilge pump. After a while, I gave up staring at my own dim reflection in the windshield. There was nothing to see beyond it, only blackness. I kept my eyes riveted to the compass.

It was 5 A.M. when I went below to awaken the captain.

The night had passed uneventfully; I hadn't seen a light or heard a sound during the entire time I was at the wheel.

George wrote on his pad, "Can you cook?"

I shook my head "No." I lied. I decided that was one job I'd avoid if at all possible. I didn't relish being confined in a tiny, musty galley below deck on a rolling sea. Not that I'd ever been seasick; I just didn't want to take the chance of getting sick. My experiences below deck on the *Dorothy K* had taught me to stay in the open air as much as possible, especially in heavy weather.

George made a most enjoyable breakfast of bacon, eggs, muffins, and coffee. I think the hot meal lifted both our spirits; I know it did mine. I looked forward to the day with great anticipation.

By daylight we were twelve hours, or about a hundred miles, out in the Gulf. While I stayed at the wheel, George brought out the sounding lead that he used to ascertain the type of bottom we were sailing over. The sounding lead weighed about five pounds. It was about two inches in diameter, ten inches long, and had a concave recess in its bottom, which was filled with yellow Kirkman soap. I throttled down the motor, and George leaned over the side and heaved the lead line as far forward as his strength would carry it. He quickly payed out the line as the lead sank to the bottom. The line was graduated in various colors, each color indicating a depth of six fathoms. By the time the lead hit bottom, it was straight down alongside the boat. George bounced it on the bottom a few times, then hauled it up, hand over hand. He studied the soap in the bottom of the lead; it contained sand. The colored line indicated we had about twenty-five fathoms of water under us. George indicated to me to head further west. We traveled for another half hour and again used the sounding lead. This time, when the line was retrieved, flecks of black, pink, and white coral appeared in the yellow soap. George nodded his head in satisfaction. We were over a coral bed.

While I swung the *Clara* in a fifty-yard circle, George broke out the anchor. The anchor was a heavily weighted grappling hook, which was dropped over the stern, rather than off the bow, as one would expect. The grappling hook would catch and hold in the coral bed and could be dislodged only by pulling it over backwards. Once the anchor was dislodged, it was not necessary to haul it up; the forward speed of the boat held it up off the bottom until we stopped again.

Our fishing rig consisted of a heavy, tarred line, identical with that which we'd used trolling for blues off Long Island when I was a boy. The line was weighted with a two-pound lead sinker; there were two large hooks to each line, baited with squares of salted filet of ladyfish. George and I each baited four lines and dropped them overboard.

It did not take long; in fact, my first line had hardly hit bottom, about a hundred and eighty feet down, when I felt a hard tug on the baited hook. I hauled the line in hand over hand as fast as I could. By the time the fish hit the surface, it was dead, or nearly so. The extreme change in pressure from the depths to the surface had caused the fish literally to explode inside. Almost all its insides were protruding from its mouth. I hauled the fish over the rail. It was a red grouper, weighing about fifteen pounds.

For the next two hours both George and I were kept busy. No sooner would we haul in a fish, sometimes two on one line, than one of our other lines would have a fish on it. There were a number of red snapper mingled with the grouper, which pleased us no end, since the snapper were our "money" fish.

And then, suddenly, the fish stopped biting. We waited about fifteen minutes; then George signaled for me to pull in my lines. We were going to move. George swung the *Clara* in a wide circle and maneuvered so that we pulled the grappling hook over backwards, dislodging it from the coral. It came loose easily.

We ran for almost an hour, seemingly on a random course, slowing down at intervals to sound with the lead. George was looking for another coral bed, but it was a good hour and a half before we located one. We set the grappling hook, and the fishing started again, with as much success as before. On this occasion, too, the fish stopped biting after a couple of hours, and we moved. Again it took an hour and a half to locate the next coral bed.

For the life of me, I could not see why George insisted on moving each time there was a lull in the fishing. Apparently, the schools of grouper and red snapper used the coral beds for their feeding grounds. They fed over one bed for a while, then moved on to another. Meanwhile, we roamed the ocean trying to locate a coral bed by guess and by gosh and by sounding lead. It seemed to me we wasted a lot of time and gasoline by moving when we might have done just as well, perhaps better, if we had sat on top of good feeding grounds and waited for the fish to come to us. This idea was purely theoretical on my part; I never got the chance to put it into practice.

We worked that day until dark. All told, we'd handlined about three hundred pounds of fish and must have spent four hours, at least, just cruising around looking for coral beds.

We had steak for supper that night. I was hungry enough to eat a grouper raw. I thought our workday was completed by the time supper was over. It wasn't, though. We spent the next three hours gutting the fish we'd caught, shoveling two thousand pounds of ice out of the fish box into the walkways, laying the fish in the bottom of the fish box, then shoveling the ice back into the box again. It was midnight when the work was finished. Believe me, I was "bushed," but I still could not fall into my bunk. George insisted, and rightly, that I sit on the stern deck for half an hour and listen for the sound of a boat whistle, a fog horn, or the rumble of a heavy motor—anything that would indicate the presence of a steamship or ocean liner. He explained the reason for such a precaution by writing notes and using signs.

The Gulf of Mexico is crisscrossed by unmarked lanes that are used constantly by passenger and freight steamers traveling to the various ports of North Florida, Louisiana, and Texas. These vessels usually travel on automatic pilot at speeds up to forty knots, in both daylight and darkness. They maintain a lookout at all times, but it seems most unlikely that a sailor on watch duty would see our tiny anchor light shining dully from the cabin roof. Of course, the ship lanes were plainly marked on the nautical charts we carried, but—where were we? We had no way of knowing. George's most educated guess could be only an approximation at best.

So I sat, in alert silence, listening for some sound that would indicate a boat nearby, straining my eyes into the darkness, looking for a light. I saw nothing but dark green waves rolling past and under our boat, then disappearing in the blackness that surrounded us. I heard nothing but the swishing of those waves and the sloshing, slapping sound they made as they hit the *Clara*'s stern transom. I looked up at the sky. Tiny, winking stars were everywhere, their brightness accentuated by the black sky. I felt lonely and insignificant. I wished I had a radio; at least I could get a weather report for the next day. I mentioned it to George. He indicated that he couldn't hear it anyway, so why bother having a radio aboard? He wrote a note saying the barometer was steady; we would have nice weather tomorrow.

When George was satisfied that I'd spent enough time watching and listening, he indicated to me I could get some sack time—but not too much. He handed me an alarm clock and told me to set it for 2 A.M. then again at 4, and again at 6. I would have to get up at two-hour intervals in order to pump out the bilge. He wrote that he was sorry, but I would have to be the one who got up, since he couldn't hear the alarm when it sounded.

The following morning, Tuesday, we started fishing soon after six. The day was like the previous one: we fished, we hunted coral beds, we fished some more. The night was a repetition of the night before. I was George's ears, listening for strange sounds, always alert for dangers that might descend upon us from any direction. We now had about seven hundred pounds of fish in our fish box, staying chilled beneath those hundreds of pounds of ice. That night, just before we retired, George pointed to the barometer. It was falling. I looked at him quizzically, but George merely shrugged.

I was rudely awakened Wednesday morning at about five o'clock by being thrown violently from my bunk. The *Clara* was pitching and tossing from side to side, and end to end. I'd noticed the sea and wind rising during the night when I was playing nursemaid to the bilge pump, but now the wind was blowing at gale force, and the waves had grown to what seemed to be gigantic proportions. The *Clara* still lay stern to the onrushing waves, riding on the grappling hook. Each wave that viciously slapped her stern dumped gallons of water over the transom into the cockpit. At the rate we were taking on water, it would be only a matter of time before we were swamped.

I awakened George, and, in the darkness, we proceeded to transfer the anchor line from the stern to the forward deck. I climbed up on the cabin roof, where I lay flat on my belly and clung desperately to the handrail to keep from being thrown overboard. George passed me a coil of the anchor rope, and I managed to get it secured to the bow cleat. I signaled to George when the line was secured, and he then loosened the rope from the stern cleat. I remained lying prone on the top deck, spread-eagled, with my fingers and toes wrapped around the handrail. I knew what would happen when the *Clara* broached broadside to the waves as she swung on the anchor line to head into the wind. She did as I expected. An especially large, white-crested wave rushed down on us just as we lay broadside. The *Clara* rolled on her round bottom until I thought the deck I lay on must be perpendicular to the black water. I tried to melt into the deck; I was sure the *Clara* couldn't possibly right herself again. She did, though, and we rode head-on into the waves. I crawled back into the stern cockpit. It was not possible to stand upright; the howling wind and the constant pitching of the boat made it more comfortable to crawl on hands and knees from one end of the cockpit to the other. I looked at George and grinned halfheartedly.

"Are you afraid?" he wrote.

"No more than you are, I guess," I answered.

"Don't worry," George wrote. "When the moon rises, the sea will become calm. We will have moonrise in a few hours."

I looked at him skeptically, but his words proved to be true. The moon rose in the east, pale and full, at about ten o'clock that morning, and almost immediately there was a perceptible decrease in the wind velocity. The sky, which had been ominously filled with scudding billows of white clouds, brightened considerably, and we were able to stand upright and look around us. The seas were still running very heavy, but they were no longer whitecapped. We got ready for breakfast and another day's fishing.

We did well our third day out. In spite of the fact that George spent as much time hunting coral beds with his sounding lead as we did fishing, we added another four or five hundred pounds of fish to the box.

The novelty and excitement of this new type of fishing wore off quickly after those three days. I enjoyed hand-lining the big grouper and snapper; often I'd have fish on all four lines at once. The time spent in actual fishing passed quickly; it was the endless hours spent cruising haphazardly looking for coral that drove me up the wall. "What a waste of time! There must be a better way to find fish," I thought.

George was a pleasant enough fellow to be with and a good all-around seaman. With the equipment he had on board, or perhaps I should say the lack of equipment, he ran his boat "by the seat of his pants," and I felt pretty safe with him in charge. I didn't work *for* George, I worked *with* him, and I liked that.

It's difficult to describe what it is like to be in the company of a deaf-mute for days on end, without the occasional relief of having someone to talk to or even a voice on a radio to listen to. I'm not exaggerating when I say that the silence was overwhelming, especially at night when George and I ate our evening meal or worked side by side gutting fish or shoveling ice in and out of the fish box in absolute silence. I'll admit that after the third day I was talking to myself, aloud, just to hear the sound of a human voice. This was particularly true during the times I sat on the stern deck alone, listening for the sound of boats.

It was with a sense of relief that I read George's note that Friday noon saying we would leave for home at about three o'clock. Our fish box was filled, the ice was almost gone, and our gas tanks were dangerously low. We'd come to the end of the expedition, for this time out, anyway.

We hauled in the grappling hook at just about the time George had planned. I took the wheel and asked him to indicate on the compass what course he wished me to follow. He pointed to northeast by east.

"How in hell does he know?" I asked myself, aloud.

"Here we've been wandering over half the Gulf of Mexico for five days, our compass is so screwed up even it doesn't know where north is, and this joker points in one direction and says 'that's the way home'! One of us has got to have rocks in his head!"

I held the *Clara* on a steady course, northeast by east. We rode a following sea and made good time, but we still had about a hundred and twenty-five miles to go, about twelve hours riding time.

It was just 3 A.M. when I saw a faint light flashing in the distance. It was still far away; it looked like a star blinking on the horizon. I grabbed George's arm and pointed to the light. George grinned and wrote on his pad: "Nokomis Inlet beacon." I was absolutely amazed. He'd hit the inlet right on the nose, purely by instinct. My opinion of my captain rose appreciably.

As we approached the landing at the fish house, we could see lights in the cottages across the canal. We could see the silhouettes of men standing on a small dock; one seemed to be shining a flashlight up into his face, and I could tell that the man's hand was raised in front of the light. George took our flashlight and did the same thing. They began to talk back and forth in sign language across the wide expanse of darkness.

I got a few hours sleep that Saturday morning before George awakened me to help unload our catch. I was glad to be back again; it felt good to have solid ground beneath my feet.

George figured our profit after we'd unloaded and weighed our catch. We had brought in two thousand pounds, worth about three hundred dollars. The owner of the *Clara*, George's brother-in-law, got a third of the gross, or one hundred dollars. Our expenses, including bait, fuel, and food, came to a hundred and twenty, leaving eighty dollars to be divided between us. George smiled as he handed me forty dollars. He wrote, "You worked very hard, and you are a good fisherman. I would like you to go out fishing with me again, if you want to."

"I would like that," I answered. "When do we sail again?"

"Sunday evening," he wrote.

This gave me a full day to drive to Jensen Beach, pick up my family, and return to Nokomis by loading time. Somehow I accomplished it, and Sunday afternoon I was at the fish house prepared to ice up for another week of fishing.

The same fishermen I'd seen the week before were in the fish house awaiting their turn to load up. This time, instead of ignoring me completely, they went out of their way to nod, or smile, or give me a salutatory "Hi-ya." Apparently they knew I'd fished with George all week, and, to a limited extent, they were willing to accept me as one of them. I noticed one peculiar thing that Sunday. The men were going through the motions of activity, but there was no loading going on. Everyone seemed to be marking time. I asked one of the captains if there was any trouble. He pointed to the blackboard: there was nothing written on it. Ted, the fish house manager, emerged from his cubbyhole of an office and walked to the blackboard. He wrote: Grouper—7¢. Snapper—15¢.

"O.K. fellas," he called to the fishermen scattered about the big room, "here's what you been waitin' on. Let's go now!"

No one made a move toward the boats. They milled

around the room talking among themselves. They ignored Ted, who stood at the blackboard looking searchingly at their faces.

"O.K. you guys—let's go fishin' now; here's what you want, good solid prices!" There was a hint of desperation in Ted's voice.

No one paid any attention to him. Ted walked hurriedly to his office and closed the door. We could see him through the glass window, telephoning. When he emerged, he walked to the board, erased the prices he had written, and wrote: Grouper—8¢. Snapper—17¢. The fishermen continued to ignore him. Now there was silence in the big room.

"There y'are, boys; it's the best I can do. How about you, Blackie? You're first in line. Let's get that ice aboard!"

The man singled out by Ted to be spokesman for the group was Captain Greg Adamos, called Blackie by the other fishermen. He was captain of the *Moon Mist*, a forty-foot converted sailing sloop. Blackie had been a sponge diver at Tarpon Springs until he got the bends once too often. He was only twenty-three years old, but looked twice that age. They said his insides were crushed; he wasn't able to eat a decent meal, but lived on crackers and milk—and bicarbonate of soda. He was forbidden ever to dive again.

"We ain't sailin', Ted. We don't like your prices." Ted was well aware that Blackie was speaking for all the fishermen.

"I'll see what I can do," Ted murmured, and walked back into the office. His face showed anxiety.

This time it was almost thirty minutes before Ted returned. We could see him through the glass, using two phones at the same time, dialing different wholesale commission agents to see if he could get better prices. At last he returned to the floor. Ted erased the previous prices and wrote in large numbers: Grouper—10¢. Snapper—20¢.

"Let's go, crew," Blackie called loudly. "What're we waitin' for?"

Blackie had spoken for us all. The loading process started with a will.

I stood by, fascinated by the events I'd just seen. I had witnessed the workings of an all-powerful labor union among men who had never actually organized. They paid no dues, they had no officers, they had written no bylaws. Yet, through Blackie, their spokesman, they had made their legitimate demands and had held out, to a man, until those demands were met. I admired their organization, which was not an organization at all.

I believe it was after my third or fourth trip with Captain George on the *Clara* that I had a chance to spend an hour or so in conversation with the captains and crews of the other boats. We were all gathered in the fish house on a Sunday afternoon awaiting the delivery of twenty tons of ice from the local ice house. The other fishermen had accepted me by this time, and I felt at ease with them.

"Say, fellas," I said, opening the conversation, "I've been wondering about a few things concerning the way we fish out there. Maybe you can set me straight."

"What's on your mind, Curt?" Blackie asked.

"Well, for one thing, this idea of using a sounding lead to find coral. It's such a hit and miss proposition, and I know damn well George and I spend as much time sounding for coral as we do fishing. Just this past week I went into that marine supply house on Main Street in Sarasota, and I saw one of those depth recorders, fish finders they call them, that not only shows you what kind of bottom you're sailing over, but can pick up a school of fish thirty fathoms down. Why, hell, with one of those gadgets on board you'd know every time you passed over a coral bed."

"That a fact?" Blackie's voice was noncommittal. "What else is on your mind?"

"Any of you guys ever see a direction finder? We sail out of here in a generally westerly direction, we run ten-twelve hours, and we figure our boats are doing ten knots. So by fishing time, we're maybe a hundred and twenty miles out. But where? What about wind and tide drift? Then, for the next five or six days, we're wandering all over God's Little Acre in every direction on the compass looking for coral beds. I'll bet there ain't one of us could pinpoint our location on a chart within twenty miles."

"'The Dummy ever fail to get you back to port?" one of the other men asked.

I knew he referred to George. "Dummy" was a nickname given to him without malice because of his affliction.

"He always hits the inlet beacon right on the nose, day or night," I admitted. "He's got more built-in instinct in the ass of his pants than a homing pigeon!"

The fishermen laughed. They seemed to be enjoying the conversation; what I didn't know was that they were building me up for a letdown.

"Go on, kid," Blackie said, grinning, "tell us some more."

"How about the steamer lanes crisscrossing all over the Gulf, a hundred miles out?" I demanded. "Every time you anchor for the night, you can never be sure you aren't smack-dab in the middle of one."

The boys became serious: "What can we do about it?" one asked.

"Well," I replied, "a direction finder would let you pin-point on the chart exactly where you are at any given time. You pick up three different radio beams on shore; you triangulate on the chart the direction from which the beam sounds are coming; then, where the lines meet is right where you are. Your chart shows where the steamer lanes are; if the triangulation shows you're in one of the lanes, you get the hell out of there in a hurry before setting your hook for the night.

"There's one other thing that'd make it a lot safer out there," I continued. "Suppose every boat were equipped with a ship-to-ship, ship-to-shore radio? If one of us got engine trouble, or any kind of trouble for that matter, one of the other boats would pick him up on the radio and probably be able to help out. The Coast Guard is always handy, near as your radio, in case you ever need them."

No one replied to my long-winded speech for several minutes. I thought they were giving my words serious consideration. Finally Blackie said, solemnly:

"Curt, baby, maybe you got a point; maybe you got several points, in fact. But let me tell you somethin' that maybe you don't know. We fish like our daddies fished, and their daddies before them. They didn't have none of them new-fangled gadgets on board their boats, some of 'em only had sail, 'stead of motors, and yet they went fishin', day in, day out, and they come home again; at least most of 'em did. And they got their fair share of fish, same as we do. I reckon what was good enough for my daddy, and his daddy, is good enough for me!"

The other fishermen nodded their heads in agreement. It seemed I was in the minority, so I shut up. I guess I still had a lot to learn about Florida fishermen.

In later conversations with the men at the fish house, I heard stories of boats that went out for a week's fishing and were never seen or heard from again. Boats and their crews disappeared as completely as though the sea had opened up and swallowed them. Never once was there even a piece of wreckage or equipment found to indicate what fate had befallen them. The fishermen told me that the fleet had lost two or three boats each year for the past several years. Speculation had it that the boats must have been demolished during the night by fast-moving ocean liners. Whatever wreckage remained was probably sucked under by the great propellers as they passed over it. The sharks probably took care of the crew.

These stories made a lasting impression on me. I began to wonder if it was worth it—for forty or fifty dollars a week.

The owners of the fish house at Nokomis purchased and outfitted a brand new fifty-foot boat, which they believed would be a fine addition to the fleet. This new boat was diesel-powered, fast, and as seaworthy as any boat in the fleet. Ted was given command of her, an assignment which pleased him greatly since he was tired of managing the fish house. It had been many years since Ted had sailed, and he was unfamiliar with that vast expanse of ocean with its scattered coral beds, better hidden than eggs at Easter time. It was arranged that George and I in the *Clara* would lead the new boat to the fishing grounds.

Both boats left on Sunday afternoon as usual. We sailed all night, arriving at the first coral bed about 5 A.M. It was a large bed, and Ted's boat, the *Sea Witch*, anchored over the same bed, but a few hundred yards off our port side.

We caught large grouper for about two hours, pulling them in one after another. Then, as usual, they suddenly stopped biting. The school had wandered off to other feeding grounds. George signaled to Ted on the *Sea Witch* that we were moving on to find another coral bed. When Ted tried to start the big diesel, the starter motor failed to work. He signaled for us to come alongside.

George and I climbed aboard the *Sea Witch* and joined Ted and his partner Steve in the engine room. We soon discovered that the starter's Bendix spring had broken in half. There was no way to repair it and no other way we could get the motor started.

The *Clara* took the *Sea Witch* in tow, and we started the long journey back to port. George and Ted were aboard the *Clara*; Steve and I remained aboard the *Sea Witch*. The little *Clara* labored under the heavy load she towed astern. She was not able to make more than five knots an hour.

We finally made it to Nokomis Inlet. Thank goodness the seas remained comparatively calm and the wind continued blowing gently from the west. After the *Sea Witch* and *Clara* had been moored at the loading dock, Ted called me into the office. He motioned me to take a chair in front of the desk.

"Your fishin' trip was cut short because of me and my boat," he said. "You wasted gas, bait, ice, maybe even some of the food George put aboard. All this will have to be paid for out of your next trip. How do you feel about that?"

"I think we're lucky we were able to get the *Sea Witch* back home safely," I replied. "That little *Clara's* got more guts in her than I gave her credit for. So far as the food, gas, and stuff is concerned, we didn't lose much—only a little money. What is important, we got you home safe. Maybe next time it'll be us out there needing a tow. I'd hate to think any one of the fleet would leave us out there helpless just so's they could catch a few fish."

Ted nodded and smiled. "I kinda thought you'd feel that way, but I had to be sure. I wouldn't want you to think of your pocketbook first, and the life of another fisherman second. Thanks, Curt."

We shook hands. I felt that now I was accepted without reservation by this unusual breed of men who risked their lives every day in the only trade they knew, commercial fishing.

I believe I made four or five more trips with George on the *Clara*; then, suddenly, I quit. I had gotten my belly full. I'd had it! My decision was a surprise to George and the other fishermen, but I meant to stick to it.

I've thought about it many times since that last trip, trying to pinpoint just what it was that made me decide to give up fishing. Perhaps it was a vague, uneasy premonition of disaster or a fear of those dangers that hung over us constantly, like a sword of Damocles. I thought about the responsibility I had to Evelyn and the kids. The idea of being away from my family for a week or so at a time, then home for a day or two, then back to sea again, did not rest well with my conscience. I think it was the loneliness that finally got to me. George was a fine, intelligent man; I admired him greatly, but, because we could never talk, or even carry on an extended written conversation, I felt completely alone out there, with only my own thoughts and words spoken aloud for companionship.

I felt sure that I could do better for my family financially. Actually, on the *Clara*, I worked sixteen hours a day, six days a week, for an average of forty dollars. This meant that I was working for about forty cents an hour. I made up my mind that my wife and kids deserved more than I was able to give them as a grouper fisherman.

Reluctantly, I helped Evelyn pack up our few belongings and the children. We were going back to New York, where I'd make a fresh start. I didn't want to leave Florida—I'd gotten sand in my shoes and felt the warm Gulf breeze on my face, and I knew I'd never be happy until I returned. I made a solemn vow to myself that someday I'd be back and I'd return to fishing. Perhaps the next time I would not be deterred or discouraged by the inevitable lot of the commercial fisherman—a wet butt and a hungry gut.

# 11 ~ One More Rainbow

TWENTY YEARS have gone by since I stepped ashore from the *Clara* and bid good-bye to Captain George and the men of the Nokomis fishing fleet. Twenty years! At times it seems as if it were only yesterday.

I returned to New York with my family and set out to find a niche for myself in the business world, for my family's sake. I do not hesitate to say that I had only mediocre success, although, as is always the case, the definition of the word "success" is relative.

I remained "up North" for ten years, but my heart had stayed in Florida, while my physical self fought the battle of icy roads, slushy, dirty snow, hot summer pavements, and the polite sham of business society. I found it almost impossible to control my feet, itching to head south, back to the land I'd grown to love.

The opportunity finally came for me in the early '60's to achieve my desire of returning to Florida. My children were grown and on their own; Evelyn, too, had found what I sincerely hope were greener pastures; and I was free to return to being the "Florida boy" I had never outgrown.

Now, another ten years have gone by. During the past decade I have not returned to commercial fishing, as perhaps you thought I would. Instead, I've continued in the business world, a dry-land sailor, with one eye on the business at hand but the other eye constantly looking towards the bays and the open sea, looking for that last rainbow, not with a pot of gold at its end, but a fishing boat.

Every man must have his dream, his rainbow. Without it,

life becomes intolerable; we cease to live as men and become vegetables. My dream is a living, driving force that sustains and excites me during these few short months that must elapse before I can fulfill that dream.

There is a place, almost too small to be seen on the map, called Pine Island. It is off the West Coast of Florida, about eighteen miles due west of Fort Myers. Pine Island is only sparsely inhabited. Its waterways are still clean, unspoiled, in their natural state, not yet scarred beyond redemption by dredges, land-fill operations, and artificial yacht basins. The land, with its stands of loblolly pine and dense mangrove forests, is still virgin, playing host to the eagles and ospreys in its tall trees, furry creatures that live unmolested in the shaded undergrowth, and, in the bays that surround the island, fish teem by the millions, oysters and clams grow plump and fat in the clean-washed shallows. Across the bay from Pine Island are Redfish Pass and Captiva Pass, which give access to the open sea. Legend tells of pirate ships that plied their trade in the Gulf waters off the coast and used Captiva Pass to enter the inland coves and bays, where they were safely hidden from the English, French, and Spanish navies. Captiva Island was the place where ill-gotten booty was buried, and where captured women of nobility and wealth were held awaiting payment of ransom. I believe that if Captain Jean Lafitte or José Gaspar were to return today, they would find little change in the waters or islands they knew a century and a half ago.

On the road leading to Pine Island, on the shores of San Carlos Bay, lies the little fishing village of Matlacha (Mat-la-shay). None of the buildings in town stand more than a single story high. Most of them are built on pilings, their back ends jutting out over the clear, sparkling waters of the bay. The shoreline is dotted with commercial fish houses, and on almost any day except Sunday the little harbor is alive with gill-net fishermen, oystermen, and crab-trappers scurrying back and forth in their little boats, unloading their night's catch at the fish house docks, or sitting quietly in the shade of the coconut palms mending their nets.

There is a general store in Matlacha, a barber shop, a post office, a Baptist Church, a couple of beer joints, and two family-style restaurants. Oh, yes, connected to one of the beer joints is a little, wood-frame hotel with eight rooms. The hotel, dubbed the Matlacha Hilton by some tourist from the North, is built on wooden pilings, with the entire building extending out over the water. On stormy nights and during high tides, one is actually rocked to sleep as the building sways gently with the motion of the sea.

I think it is the people of the little village that attract me most. They're simple folk, about fifty years behind the times, by modern standards. They have not yet learned how to deliberately pollute the air and clean waters nature has given them. They have not yet learned how to steal from one another, or how to attack and abuse the elderly and defenseless among them. They have not yet become so selfish that they place the possession of wealth above all other virtues. They are not so busy that they cannot take time to help one another. Yes, indeed, the people of Matlacha are way behind the times. They are Florida fishermen, and I yearn with all my heart to be one of them once more.

Step by step, literally inch by inch, I am getting closer to my rainbow's end. I've acquired a piece of land on Pine Island and will move to it in just a little while. I've bought a little fishing boat, too, which will be ideal for almost any type of commercial fishing in Pine Island Sound. She is sixteen feet long, lapstraked, with a six-foot beam. Built like a dory, she's wide and safe and sturdy. She reminds me of another dory I once owned. What will I name her? Why, she'll be the *Trickey III*, of course!

Each week I accumulate some article of gear or equipment I think I'll need to start my new venture. My mobile home is already cluttered with anchors, rope, crab traps, gill nets, and all sorts of fishing tackle. Some of the things I've bought are not new, and the smell of the sea still clings to them, tempting me, enticing me to put them to use. Oftentimes, during the evening hours, I sit studying a chart of the waters surrounding Pine Island. In my mind's eye, I choose the spots where mullet might feed, the deep holes where snook would lie, or the tide runs where my gill net might catch the wary trout.

Will I make a success of it this time? As Jean Lafitte would say: "Qui sait?" Again, the word "success" is only relative. If success means wealth, social prestige, and accumulated possessions, no, I will not be successful. If it means that I have found contentment, peace of mind, and happiness derived from the bounties that God and nature have set before me, yes, I will have found success; for, after all, will I not have found the end of my rainbow?